Best Climbs
Tahquitz and Suicide Rocks

BOB GAINES

FALCONGUIDES

GUILFORD, CONNECTICUT
HELENA, MONTANA

AN IMPRINT OF ROWMAN & LITTLEFIELD

WARNING

Climbing is a sport where you may be seriously injured or die. Read this before you use this book.

This guidebook is a compilation of unverified information gathered from many different climbers. The author cannot ensure the accuracy of any of the information in this book, including the topos and route descriptions, the difficulty ratings, and the protection ratings. These may be incorrect or misleading, as ratings of climbing difficulty and danger are always subjective and depend on the physical characteristics (for example, height), experience, technical ability, confidence, and physical fitness of the climber who supplied the rating. Additionally, climbers who achieve first ascents sometimes underrate the difficulty or danger of the climbing route. Therefore, be warned that you must exercise your own judgment on where a climbing route goes, its difficulty, and your ability to safely protect yourself from the risks of rock climbing. Examples of some of these risks are: falling due to technical difficulty or due to natural hazards such as holds breaking, falling rock, climbing equipment dropped by other climbers, hazards of weather and lightning, your own equipment failure, and failure or absence of fixed protection.

You should not depend on any information gleaned from this book for your personal safety; your safety depends on your own good judgment, based on experience and a realistic assessment of your climbing ability. If you have any doubt as to your ability to safely climb a route described in this book, do not attempt it.

The following are some ways to make your use of this book safer:

1. Consultation: You should consult with other climbers about the difficulty and danger of a particular climb prior to attempting it. Most local climbers are glad to give advice on routes in their area; we suggest that you contact locals to confirm ratings and safety of particular routes and to obtain firsthand information about a route chosen from this book.

2. Instruction: Most climbing areas have local climbing instructors and guides available. We recommend that you engage an instructor or guide to learn safety techniques and to become familiar with the routes and hazards of the areas described in this book. Even after you are proficient in climbing safely, occasional use of a guide is a safe way to raise your climbing standard and learn advanced techniques.

3. Fixed Protection: Some of the routes in this book may use bolts and pitons that are permanently placed in the rock. Because of variances in the manner of placement, weathering, metal fatigue, the quality of the metal used, and many other factors, these fixed protection pieces should always be considered suspect and should always be backed up by equipment that you place yourself. Never depend on a single piece of fixed protection for your safety, because you never can tell whether it will hold weight. In some cases, fixed protection may have been removed or is now missing. However, climbers should not always add new pieces of protection unless existing protection is faulty. Existing protection can be tested by an experienced climber and its strength determined. Climbers are strongly encouraged not to add bolts and drilled pitons to a route. They need to climb the route in the style of the first ascent party (or better) or choose a route within their ability—a route to which they do not have to add additional fixed anchors.

Be aware of the following specific potential hazards that could arise in using this book:

1. Incorrect Descriptions of Routes: If you climb a route and you have a doubt as to where it goes, you should not continue unless you are sure that you can go that way safely. Route descriptions and topos in this book could be inaccurate or misleading.

2. Incorrect Difficulty Rating: A route might be more difficult than the rating indicates. Do not be lulled into a false sense of security by the difficulty rating.

3. Incorrect Protection Rating: If you climb a route and you are unable to arrange adequate protection from the risk of falling through the use of fixed pitons or bolts and by placing your own protection devices, do not assume that there is adequate protection available higher just because the route protection rating indicates the route does not have an X or an R rating. Every route is potentially an X (a fall may be deadly), due to the inherent hazards of climbing—including, for example, failure or absence of fixed protection, your own equipment's failure, or improper use of climbing equipment.

There are no warranties, whether expressed or implied, that this guidebook is accurate or that the information contained in it is reliable. There are no warranties of fitness for a particular purpose or that this guide is merchantable. Your use of this book indicates your assumption of the risk that it may contain errors and is an acknowledgment of your own sole responsibility for your climbing safety.

Contents

Tahquitz and Suicide Rocks Overview

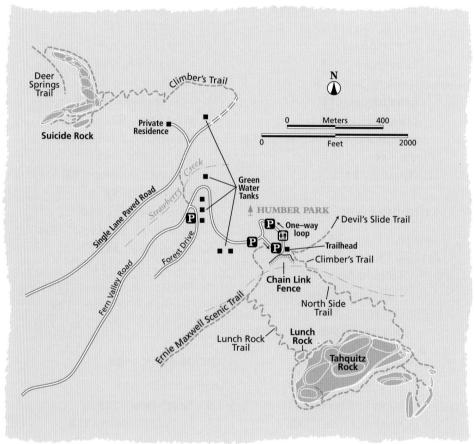

Acknowledgments

First of all I'd like to thank John Burbidge at FalconGuides/Globe Pequot Press for putting it all together. Great thanks to Darrell Hensel for his info and comments. Darrell has been THE local Suicide Rock slab master for decades, and his knowledge of Suicide Rock is unsurpassed. Special thanks to Kelly Vaught for providing detailed new route information, topos, photos, and notes. In addition to putting up many excellent new routes, Kelly has climbed more routes at Tahquitz and Suicide than anyone, and his knowledge of the area is remarkable. Thanks to Randy Vogel and Chuck Wilts for paving the way with their excellent series of Tahquitz and Suicide guidebooks. Thanks to John Long for editing the history section. Thanks to Charlie Peterson and Tommy Romero for teaming up with me for all those fun first ascents. I'd like to thank Kevin Powell and Greg Epperson for their great climbing photographs. Thanks to Erik Roed in particular for all his new route information and route details. Thanks to Frank Bentwood, Alan Bartlett, Clark Jacobs, John Weinberg, Tony Sartin, Todd Gordon, Dave Mayville, Tony Grice, Erik Kramer-Webb, Wendell Smith, and Brad Young for providing route information and descriptions, drawing topos, and fielding all my questions on specific route details. Thanks to my wife, Yvonne, for being my best climbing partner—her first climb on Tahquitz was when she accompanied me on the first free ascent of *The Bat*, in 1987!

Kay Okamoto leads pitch three of *El Camino Real* (5.10a) Photo Greg Epperson

Introduction

Tahquitz and Suicide Rocks are located high above the picturesque mountain town of Idyllwild, California, in the upper reaches of pine-forested Fern Valley. Tahquitz Rock is a 1,000-foot-high dome of granite jutting out from the west flank of Tahquitz Peak. The summit of Tahquitz Rock is about 8,000 feet in elevation. Climbs on Tahquitz are predominantly multi-pitch trad climbs, averaging three to seven pitches in length, following vertical crack systems. On the faces and buttresses between the cracks are a number of excellent bolt-protected slab climbs and a few steep face climbs.

Directly across Fern Valley from Tahquitz Rock is Suicide Rock, a long cliff band that contours nearly a mile of mountainside, facing predominantly south and east. Suicide Rock has a complex, multi-faceted structure, with numerous cliffs, slabs, buttresses, and blocky pinnacles, all with excellent rock quality and climbs ranging from one to three pitches in length and up to 400 feet high. Suicide Rock is known for its world-class slab climbs, but has an assortment of excellent crack climbs as well. The summit is a broad, flat area at an elevation of about 7,500 feet.

Called "Lily Rock" on topo maps, climbers have long referred to it as Tahquitz Rock. The name Tahquitz is derived from Indian legend. According to Native American folklore, the rock covers the doorway to the cave of Tahquitch, the Indian equivalent of the devil, and rumblings within the rock signify Tahquitch's displeasure . There is some disagreement as to the correct pronunciation. It is most commonly pronounced by climbers as either TAH-keets, or tah-QUITZ.

How to Get to Idyllwild

From West LA/San Fernando Valley: Take I-10 east to the town of Banning, then head south on Highway 243. From here it is 25 miles of winding mountain road up to Idyllwild.

From South Bay and Orange County: Take the 91 Freeway east to Riverside, then exit on Van Buren Boulevard. Take Van Buren to I-215 South to the Ramona Expressway. Head east on the Ramona Expressway through the town of San Jacinto. Ramona Expressway becomes Mountain Avenue and ends at Highway 74 in the town of Hemet. Turn left onto Highway 74 and take this up

Tom Murphy leads pitch 2
of *Green Arch* (5.11c)

to Mountain Center. Turn left in Mountain Center onto Highway 243 and go 5 miles up to Idyllwild.

From San Diego: Take I-15 to I-215 North to Highway 74 east (through Hemet), then up to Mountain Center. Turn left onto Highway 243 and go 5 miles up to Idyllwild.

From Palm Springs: Take I-10 west (toward LA) to the town of Banning, then go south on Highway 243. From here it is 25 miles of winding mountain road up to Idyllwild.

Camping, Motels, and Cabins

There are two fee campgrounds located in the town of Idyllwild: Idyllwild County Park and Mount San Jacinto State Park. All campsites have fire pits and picnic tables. Both campgrounds have water and flush toilets.

Idyllwild County Park has ninety-two sites and showers. Call (800) 234-PARK (7275) for reservations up to four days in advance. Credit cards are accepted over the phone, or reserve online at www.riversidecountyparks.org.

Mount San Jacinto State Park has thirty-three sites and free showers. Call (800) 444-PARK (7275) for reservations with a credit card, at least 48 hours in advance, or reserve online at www.reserveamerica.com.

Idyllwild is a mountain resort town with a vast array of motel rooms and cabin accommodations. Most of the motels and cabin rentals have a two-night minimum on weekends. For more information on Idyllwild lodging and restaurants, visit www.idyl.com or www.idyllwild.com. For deluxe cabin rentals, contact Idyllwild Vacation Rentals at (800) 297-1410 or online at www.idyllwildvacationrentals.com.

How to Use This Guide

The "best climbs" in this book were selected based on rock quality, purity, and position of line (natural lines of weakness up the cliff); fun, interesting, unique, or noteworthy climbing; existing climber access trails; and user-friendly approaches and descents.

I have personally climbed almost every route in this book, and if not, one of my trusted friends has, and can attest to a quality climbing experience.

A quality rating system is used (one, two, or three stars) to further distinguish the value of the climbs. A one-star route is a worthwhile climb of good quality; a two-star climb is a very good or great climb of very high quality; and a three-star route is an undisputed classic, the best that Tahquitz and Suicide Rocks have to offer. Some routes with no stars (below average or average quality) are included in the text and on some topos, where that route serves as a

How to Get to Idyllwild

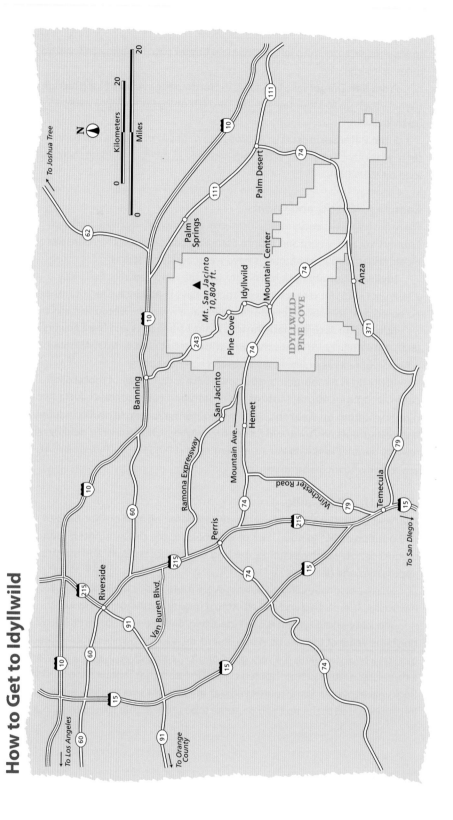

reference point to surrounding climbs, or to give you more routes to do at a particular cliff.

The routes are generally listed from left to right as you face the cliff. Directions (e.g., "go right" or "climb up and left," etc.) are given as if you are facing the route from the base or from anywhere on the route. Directions for climbing, downclimbing, descending, rappelling, etc., are given for the same orientation (as if you were facing the route from the start of the route).

On some routes, pitch lengths (e.g., 120 feet) are given; these are estimates and not exact figures. Recommended belay spots are just that—recommended— and where you decide to belay is your choice. Personally I tend to climb shorter pitches, eschewing the current trend toward longer pitches and pushing to see how few pitches a multi-pitch climb can be done in. My proclivity is due to a long career as a professional climbing guide, where I like to keep an eye on my client, and to the fact that with a lot of rope out, it's more difficult to protect a falling second from hitting a ledge because of rope stretch. Also, I despise rope drag, especially on hard, delicate slab moves.

Rappel descents less than 30 meters (98 feet) are described as "rappel 100 feet" and can be done with a standard 60-meter (200-foot) rope. Rappels over 100 feet, described as "rappel with two ropes" require two ropes, with the estimated distance usually given (e.g., rappel 165 feet). In some instances a rappel over 100 feet can be done with a single 70-meter (230-foot) rope, described as "rappel 35 meters or 115 feet. *To prevent rappelling off one or both ends of your rope, or having an accident while lowering, always close your rope system by tying knots in the ends of your rope!*

Route lines drawn on the photo topos are approximations; every effort has been made to depict the exact line of the route, but again, trust your judgment. Bolt locations on the topos are also approximations; however, in some cases the depiction of the bolt location is extremely accurate—thanks to digital photography, I often could zoom in and actually see the bolt in the photograph. In other cases the location depicted on the photo topo is the best approximation of the exact location. Fixed pins are marked on some of the topos with a "P." These signify key fixed pitons; if the piton has been removed or pulled out in a fall, the protection rating of the route may have changed to a PG or an R.

GPS coordinates are given for parking areas, trailheads, and key points along the approach trails.

In the route descriptions, trees are often used as identifying landmarks (e.g., "belay at a small ledge with a mountain mahogany"), so here's a brief tutorial on identifying the types of trees used in the route descriptions. A mountain mahogany, commonly found growing on Tahquitz Rock, is a diminutive,

Idyllwild Area Map

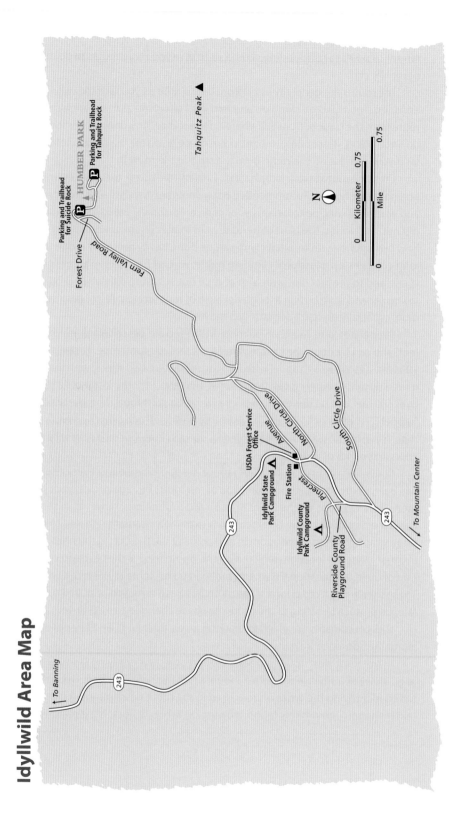

shrublike tree with a gray, furrowed trunk and olive-colored, oval-shaped leaves approximately ¼ by 1 inch in size. These small trees are generally not strong enough to be relied upon as failsafe anchors, especially when they are dead, dry, and brittle. In a few rare instances they serve as key handholds for otherwise bleak passages.

Numerous pine trees grow on the rock faces and ledges of both Tahquitz and Suicide Rocks. A fir tree is a pine with short, single needles that looks like a Christmas tree. Yellow pines (Coulter and Jeffrey) have long, 6-inch needles, three to a bundle. Sugar pines grow large at both rocks, with medium, 3-inch needles, five to a bundle. Oak trees and scrub oak also grow at both rocks.

More Route Information and New Routes
Many of the less popular or more obscure routes are not included in this book. Information on many of these routes is included in the comprehensive *Rock Climbing Tahquitz and Suicide Rocks,* 2001 edition, by Bob Gaines and Randy Vogel, published by Globe Pequot Press.

Detailed route information is also available online at www.mountainproject.com; just click on Tahquitz and Suicide Rocks. Mountain Project currently lists route descriptions for 353 routes at Tahquitz and Suicide.

In return for buying this book, I'll be glad to share with you any route information, beta, and insights I've gained over thirty-five years of climbing at Idyllwild, on any of the routes at Tahquitz or Suicide Rocks. Feel free to contact me. Also, if you have any new route information, corrections, or input, I'd be much obliged if you'd share it with me.

You can contact me at BGvertical@aol.com.

Climbing Seasons
Climbing is possible year-round at Tahquitz and Suicide Rocks, although the prime climbing season is spring, summer, and fall. Winter (December through February) weather can be sunny and cool—ideal conditions for climbing the hard face routes at the south-facing cliffs on Suicide Rock and on the great South Face of Tahquitz. The days are short, however, and if there is a cold front moving through, temperatures can remain in the 40s during the day. In the wintertime it is generally too cold to climb in the shade on the north and northwest sides of Tahquitz and in the late afternoon at Suicide Rock when the entire cliff goes into the shade. During an entire winter season, there are usually several big storms that dump up to a foot of snow above Idyllwild, leaving the approach trails blanketed in white for a week or two, and snow piled up in the shady spots at the base of the rocks. By March or April most of the snow is

usually melted, but some of the north- and northwest-facing cliffs may still have some snow at the base and the cracks may be a bit wet and dripping with water in places.

May and June are the prime months for reliably good weather, comfortable temps, and long sunny days for the big multi-pitch climbs. July and August can be too hot to climb comfortably all day on the south-facing cliffs, but the west side of Tahquitz is in the shade until almost noon and provides comfortable conditions even on the warmest summer days. Much of Suicide Rock bakes in the summer sun until about 2 or 2:30 p.m., when most of the cliff goes into the shade.

In July, August, and September, afternoon thunderstorms can develop, and sometime from late July to early September, a periodic monsoonal moisture pattern usually develops intermittently for a week or two. During this time daily thunderstorms build up, making the long routes on Tahquitz a dicey affair because of the threat of lightning. Moisture in the air and clouds streaming in from the south early in the morning is a harbinger of thunderstorms to come later in the day. If you see cumulous clouds quickly building as you make the approach to Tahquitz, beware.

The fall offers cooler temperatures and stable weather, and late September and early October weather is typically delightful, with a crispness to the air. In the late fall the angle of the sun shifts, and the North, Northwest, and West Faces of Tahquitz receive sun only late in the afternoon. By mid-October the door is open for the first cold fronts to begin blowing through, and by late October or early November, the first snowfall has often occurred.

Climbing Gear

A standard Tahquitz and Suicide rack includes a double set of nuts (stoppers or rocks, perhaps a few medium tricams or hexes) and a double set of camming devices from 0.4 to 2.5 inches, plus one 3-inch piece. A few larger cams from 3 to 5 inches are useful for some climbs where indicated. Micro-nuts (like RPs or Black Diamond Micro Stoppers) and very small camming devices and three-cam units are very useful for many of the more difficult routes.

In this book the size given (e.g., a 2-inch cam) refers to the *width of the crack,* and a camming device with a manufacturer's recommended optimal placement at 2 inches in width will best fit a 2-inch crack. A route description that lists pro as 0.4 to 1.5 inches means the *width of the cracks* are 0.4 to 1.5 inches.

A 60-meter (200-foot) rope is the standard climbing rope for Tahquitz and Suicide Rocks although a 70-meter (230-foot) rope is useful for rappelling where noted and for extending pitches on the longer routes.

Both rocks involve a fairly lengthy approach over rough trails. Good-quality approach shoes or lightweight hiking boots are recommended.

Climbing and camping equipment is available at Nomad Ventures, 54415 N. Circle Dr., Idyllwild, (951) 659-4853, www.nomadventures.com.

Climbing Safety

Safety in rock climbing involves judgment. Good judgment in rock climbing is learned over time by experience. If you are inexperienced in traditional, or "trad," climbing techniques, consider hiring a guide to gain knowledge and confidence in protection placements, anchoring fundamentals, and principals of multi-pitch climbing.

If it's your first time climbing a multi-pitch route, start by climbing well below your limit, as techniques for many routes will seem peculiar at first, and ratings will seem underrated until you are more familiar with the rock and its idiosyncrasies.

On many of the longer routes on Tahquitz, routefinding can be complex, with many options; setting up complicated gear anchors can be time-consuming; and the approach and descent may take longer than you anticipate. Get an early start, and bring a headlamp—more than a few parties have been benighted their first time out at Tahquitz.

Vertical Adventures Climbing School offers rock climbing classes at Suicide Rock and guided climbs of Tahquitz Rock. Call (800) 514-8785 or visit www.verticaladventures.com.

If the route description or topo seems wrong, it may very well be wrong—trust your instincts. Every effort has been made to provide accurate route descriptions, topos, and crack sizes for gear recommendations, but inevitably there will be inaccuracies.

If you're leading a route and it doesn't feel right, back off. You may be off-route, on the wrong route, or just having a bad day. Discretion is better than hubris. Many leader fall accidents have occurred when climbers underestimated the difficulty of a climb or their ability to place good protection.

Very few of the bolt-protected face climbs at Tahquitz or Suicide can be considered sport climbs. A majority of the face climbs, even those that are entirely bolt protected, have what most sport climbers would consider to be long runouts between bolts—runouts of 15 to 25 feet being commonplace. These routes reflect the staunch ground-up traditional ethics of the 1960s through the 1980s and into the 1990s, where on first ascents bolts were drilled on lead, by hand, and from stances (see the History section).

In the 1960s and 1970s boldness was a virtue, and many climbs from this era reflect a daring, go-for-it style that will be starkly evident when you're on the sharp end of the rope. The original ¼-inch bolts, usually drilled from extremely tenuous stances, have been replaced with new ⅜-inch or ½-inch diameter bolts, upping the safety factor, but the exhilarating runouts are still there. These routes require focus, mental control, and calmness under duress to succeed; the slightest shake or quiver of a leg and you're off, in some cases for a mighty big fall. If you're inexperienced in runout slab climbing, tread cautiously; pay your dues by starting out slow and working your way up through the grades. Idyllwild is not a sport climbing area.

Ratings of PG, R, or X are warnings that the routes have protection problems or include unprotected sections of a climb where a fall may result in injury or death. A route rated PG means that there are some protection difficulties. The pro may be difficult to place, may require advanced rigging techniques, or may simply be so far below your feet at a crux that you'll be facing a long, difficult-to-control fall if you come off, with the potential for injury. An R-rated route designates a route where a fall at the crux will be disastrous, likely resulting in very serious injury or death. An X-rated route designates a complete and utter lack of protection at a crux, where a fall will result in hitting the ground or hitting a ledge, likely resulting in death. In addition, some routes with climbing that is seriously unprotected but significantly easier than the crux are given an additional protection warning. For example, a route may be rated 5.10a but with 5.7 R noted in the route description text, meaning there is dangerously unprotected 5.7 climbing on the route, although the crux 5.10a section is relatively well protected. **Be aware that many routes have *easy sections* that are rated R or X, but are not given that designation in this book.**

Suicide Rock has relatively little loose rock, although beware when parties are topping out, as there are some cliffs (like the Weeping Wall) with precarious loose rocks on slabs near the cliff edge, easily pulled off by careless rope handling.

Tahquitz Rock, on the other hand, does have quite a few areas with loose blocks and flakes, particularly on the Northeast Face, North Face, and Northwest Recess. Several fatalities have occurred at Tahquitz due to rockfall. Test loose flakes carefully before committing to pulling on them, and be especially cautious when dealing with loose blocks. On ledges, watch where you flake your rope pile, as this can be the culprit for inadvertent rockfall. If you do knock off a loose rock, always yell "rock" to warn others who may be below you. Whether or not you choose to climb below other parties is up to you, but be aware that many rockfall accidents have occurred in this scenario, particularly on moderate routes popular with novices. Obviously, wearing a helmet is a good idea on Tahquitz.

On weekends the popular routes on Tahquitz are crowded; to avoid having to climb below another party, you simply need to start early. If you can swing it, weekdays are far less crowded and a real joy to climb on at Tahquitz, as you have your pick of routes without much competition.

As previously mentioned, fixed pins (i.e., pitons) are noted in some of the route descriptions. These may or may not be there, as some get pulled in falls or are removed as they loosen over time due to the extreme hot and cold temperatures experienced in Idyllwild. Back up fixed pins whenever possible.

Most of the routes in this book have had any old bolts replaced, although there are still some out there. If you do come across a ¼-inch bolt, trust it at your peril, especially if the hanger is rusty or has a bronze tint to it.

A few climbers, led by Clark Jacobs, Kevin Powell, Dave Mayville, and myself, have spent considerable time and effort replacing many of the old bolts in Idyllwild with upgraded stainless steel bolts and hangers. The hardware was graciously donated by the American Safe Climbing Association (ASCA). If you'd like to support the ASCA, you can contact them through their web site www.safeclimbing.org. They do great work in supporting climbers who take the initiative to upgrade aging bolts and anchors, not only in Idyllwild but also in climbing areas throughout the country, for the benefit of all climbers.

Tahquitz and Suicide Rocks have a unique set of objective hazards. Rattlesnakes are occasionally seen on the approach trails and at the base of the rocks (most commonly at the base of Suicide Rock) and are most active in warmer (80°F and up) weather conditions. Watch where you step and be aware of your surroundings. If you happen to come across a rattlesnake, don't attempt to capture or kill it; instead, give it plenty of space and it will usually slither away on its own accord. In the event of a rattlesnake bite, Loma Linda Medical Center in Loma Linda (west of Banning on I-10, 909-422-3097) is known for providing state-of-the-art treatment.

Africanized honey bees (killer bees) have established hives at Suicide Rock, typically found in hollowed-out oak trees. Hornets (locally referred to as yellowjackets), which both bite and sting, can be bothersome, particularly in very dry years. Their sting is similar in intensity to a bee sting. If you're allergic to bee stings, you should consider carrying a bee sting kit (epi pen) when climbing at Tahquitz or Suicide.

Deerflies (which bite) can be pesky during the summer months. Insect repellent containing DEET is somewhat effective in repelling them.

Emergencies

In the event of an accident, litters have been placed at both Tahquitz and Suicide to assist climbers in noncritical carryouts of an injured climber. At Tahquitz a litter has been traditionally cached below the West Face, at Lunch Rock, but sometimes goes missing for a time if it has actually been used for a rescue and not yet returned. Three litters currently are cached at Suicide Rock: one at the base of *The Pirate,* one at the base of the Weeping Wall, and one near the base of *Flower of High Rank.* If you happen to use one of the litters, please ensure that it is returned to its original location as soon as possible.

For technical rescues or other more serious emergencies, climbers are fortunate to have the services of the Riverside Mountain Rescue Unit, which can be dispatched by dialing 911. Over the years this nonprofit volunteer organization has been responsible for numerous technical rescues and helping many injured climbers. If you'd like to make a contribution to the Riverside Mountain Rescue Unit, visit their website at www.rmru.org.

Cell phone service is good at most areas of Tahquitz Rock, but cell signals are weak and unreliable at Suicide Rock from the Buttress of Cracks to the North Face. In general, if you don't have a line of sight to the town of Idyllwild, your cell phone may not work.

For minor injuries that need immediate care (cuts, sprains, etc.), the Idyllwild Health Center (54165 Pine Crest Ave., 951-659-4908) is open Monday through Friday from 8:30 a.m. to 1 p.m. and 2 to 5 p.m. (closed Saturday and Sunday). If you call when they're closed, a message will give you a pager number to call for a doctor on call.

Leave No Trace

You can practice Leave No Trace principles from the moment you step out of your car. Plan ahead and prepare. Always use the marked climber's trails where they are available. If there is no marked trail to the cliff, minimize your impact by walking on durable surfaces (i.e., a rock slab or barren ground).

If nature calls and you're far from any outhouse, deposit solid human waste well away from the base of any climbing site or creek by digging a cathole 8 inches deep. Cover and disguise the cathole when done. Pack out all toilet paper and tampons in a ziplock bag. Urinate on bare ground or rock, not plants. Urine contains salt, and animals will dig into plants to get to it.

Be courteous of other climbers. Respect the resident wildlife. Pick up all food crumbs, and don't feed any of the critters—this habituates them to human food and encourages them to beg and scavenge for food. If you're climbing a multi-pitch route and leaving your pack at the base, don't leave any food in your pack—squirrels will chew right through it to get at the food. Take all food out of your pack and put it in a thick plastic container, bear canister, or squirrel-proof mesh bag. For more information visit LNT.org.

In recent years the Idyllwild Climber's Alliance, in conjunction with The Access Fund, have been responsible for many trail building and maintenance projects.

The Idyllwild Climber's Alliance's mission is to "preserve the climbing areas of Idyllwild, to improve access to the crags, and to educate those who use the area about the issues affecting our climbing past, present, and future. We do service projects (cleanup and trail work), climb, and reach out to other climbers offering them fun and education."

For information on contributing to these organizations, contact:
Idyllwild Climber's Alliance
Jim Pinter-Lucke
jlucke@cmc.edu
(909) 267-5767

The Access Fund
www.accessfund.org

Permits and Adventure Pass
Both Tahquitz and Suicide Rocks are located in wilderness areas, although no hiking or climbing permit or trailhead registration is required for climbers.

A National Forest Adventure Pass is currently required for day-use parking at Humber Park, but not for parking at Suicide Rock. Annual and day-use Adventure Passes are available at the USDA Forest Service station in Idyllwild (54270 Pine Crest Ave., 909-659-2117) and at various retail establishments in town that display the sign ADVENTURE PASS SOLD HERE.

History

Tahquitz and Suicide Rocks are steeped in history. To climb in Idyll-wild is to tread the footsteps of legends who pushed new limits and helped invent technical climbing in the process. Arguably, the first climbs in America to be rated 5.8, 5.9, 5.10, 5.11, and 5.12 were done here. Tahquitz Rock is also the birthplace of the Yosemite Decimal System (thanks largely to Chuck Wilts), the rating system still used throughout the United States.

Chuck Wilts on *Whodunit* (5.9), 1962 Photo Tom Frost

The first climb on Tahquitz was *The Trough* (5.4), climbed in the summer of 1936, followed closely by ascents of *Angel's Fright* (5.6) and the *Fingertip Traverse* (5.5). In the 1930s there were less than a dozen climbs at Tahquitz, done primarily by members of the rock climbing section (RCS) of the Sierra Club, a noncompetitive bunch who were content repeating the same routes again and again, like ski runs on a ski mountain.

One climb from the 1930s stood out, however: the spectacular *Mechanics Route* (5.8), first led by Dick Jones in 1937, perhaps the most demanding lead in the country at the time. Even today climbers experience intense exhilaration on the route's second pitch—a runout face following sloping potholes that Dick Jones led wearing tennis shoes while lashed to a manila yachting rope.

The 1940s belongs to Chuck Wilts, author of the area's first comprehensive guidebook. His first ascents include what are now some of the rock's most heavily traveled routes: *Fingertrip* (5.7, 1946), *Left Ski Track* (5.6, 1947), and the first free ascent of *Piton Pooper* (5.7+, 1949).

The decade of the 1950s marks the reign of Royal Robbins. He began with the first free ascent of *The Open Book* in 1952, widely regarded as the first major multi-pitch climb in America to receive the 5.9 rating. This benchmark set a standard by which all other 5.9 routes are still measured against. Royal, teamed variously with Chuck Wilts, Don Wilson, Jerry Gallwas, and Tom Frost, climbed most of the moderate classics during this decade, using pitons for protection—routes that are very popular today, like *Whodunit* (5.9, 1957), *The Swallow* (5.10a, 1952), *The Long Climb* (5.8, 1952), *The Step* (5.10a, 1957), *The Jam Crack* (5.8, 1959), *Upper Royals Arch* (5.8, 1953), *Illegitimate* (5.9, 1959), and the first free ascents of *Innominate* (5.9, 1957) and *Consolation* (5.9, 1959).

When Royal and Dave Rearick bagged the first ascent of *The Vampire* (5.9, A4) in 1959, nailing pitons in the Vampire's thin and expanding flakes, it was a breakthrough and a precursor of things to come. In 1961 Royal teamed up with Tom Frost and Chuck Pratt for the first ascent of El Capitan's *Salathe Wall,* widely considered one of the greatest rock climbs of all time. Royal would go on to become one of Yosemite's preeminent big wall climbers, and one of the most talented free climbers of his generation. It all began at Tahquitz.

Royal Robbins on the third pitch of *Jonah* (5.10d) during the second ascent in 1964
PHOTO ROYAL ROBBINS COLLECTION

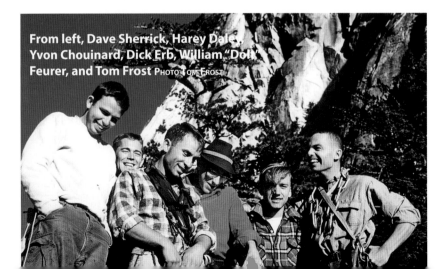

From left, Dave Sherrick, Harey Daley, Yvon Chouinard, Dick Erb, William "Dolt" Feurer, and Tom Frost PHOTO TOM FROST

Yvon Chouinard wrote about the influence Tahquitz had on Yosemite climbing in his influential article, "Modern Yosemite Climbing," published in the 1963 *American Alpine Journal.* According to Chouinard:

Yvon Chouinard at Tahquitz Rock, 1971
PHOTO BY TOM FROST

All the techniques for free climbing were established not at Yosemite, but at Tahquitz Rock in Southern California. From the 1930s to the present day, it has been a teaching ground for nearly every prominent Valley climber. This magnificent rock has over 70 routes on massive, exfoliated granite, similar to Yosemite except for the lack of glacial polish and dirt in the cracks. This means that a move will go free at Tahquitz where normally in Yosemite it would require direct aid. Because of its accessibility, compactness, and solid piton cracks, Tahquitz offers ideal conditions for pushing free climbing to its limits. Most of the routes were first done with direct aid, but over a period of time nearly every one has been done free. It was the first area to have class 5.9 climbs and continues to have the greatest concentration of 5.8, 5.9, and 5.10 routes in the country.

When one finds a layback or friction pitch at Tahquitz, it is a textbook-type pitch; a lay-back is a pure lay-back requiring pure lay-back technique, a friction pitch require pure friction technique. Nothing else will do. One can develop granite-climbing technique here far better than in Yosemite or anywhere else. I cannot impress it enough on climbers from other areas to climb Tahquitz before going to Yosemite. Every spring, even the native climbers spend a week at Tahquitz getting in shape for the Valley walls.

In the 1960s standards rose again, mainly due to the efforts of Bob Kamps. Kamps made the first ascent of the unclimbed Diamond (5.10) on Colorado's Long Peak in 1960 with Dave Rearick, and was perhaps the most talented free climber of his generation. Partnered variously with Rearick, Tom Frost, TM Herbert, and Tom Higgins, Kamps made first ascents of *The Rack* (5.10a, 1961), *Human Fright* (5.10a, 1963), *Blanketty Blank* (5.10c, 1963), and *Pearly Gate* (5.10a, 1969), among others. His dedication to free climbing led him to first free ascents of previously aided climbs, many of which are today considered classics: *The Blank* (5.10b, 1960), *El Grandote* (5.9, 1963), and *Who-dunit* (5.9, 1966). But perhaps Kamps's greatest achievement at Tahquitz was his 1967 first ascent of *Chingadera* (5.11a, originally rated 5.10), which was one of the most difficult face climbs in America at the time.

While the 1950s and 1960s were a period of great exploration at Tahquitz, Suicide Rock remained largely ignored until the late 1960s. A group of climbers led by Pat Callis, including Charlie and Trish Raymond, Lee Harrell, and Larry Reynolds, established thirty new routes at Suicide between 1966 and 1969, including such classics as *Surprise* (5.8), *Serpentine* (5.9), *David* (5.7), *Spooky Spike* (5.9), *Captain Hook* (5.8), and the ultra-classic *Sundance* (5.10b). They also nailed (with pitons) *The Pirate* (A2), *Etude* (A2), *Insomnia* (A3), and *Paisano Overhang* (A3), setting the stage for the next generation of climbers with prospects of first free ascents.

The decade of the 1970s began with a landmark climb, *Valhalla* (5.11a), done in 1970 by local climbers Ivan Couch, Larry Reynolds, and Mike Dent, setting a new standard of difficulty for Suicide Rock. But when Jim Erickson, a visiting climber from Colorado, snatched the prized first free ascent of *Insomnia Crack* (5.11b)

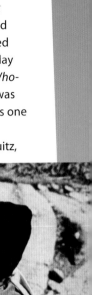

Ivan Couch on the first ascent of *Valhalla* (5.11a), 1970 PHOTO LARRY REYNOLDS

in 1972, it was a sign that the current generation was resting on its laurels.

In 1973, when Mike Graham (age 17) and Tobin Sorenson (age 18) climbed the first ascent of *New Generation* (5.11c) on Suicide's Sunshine Face, not only was it the most technically demanding route of its kind in America, but it also was a sign of things to come. A new generation of climbers would dominate the 1970s. Led by John Long, Rick Accomazzo, Richard Harrison, Mike Graham, Tobin Sorenson, John Bachar, Gib Lewis, Charles Cole, Rob Muir, Mike Lechlinski, Lynn Hill, Erik Erickson, and Bill Antel, they called themselves the "Stonemasters." To enter the club there was only one rule: You had to climb *Valhalla*.

Long was the driving force behind many of the first free ascents,

John Long on the first pitch of *Hades* (5.12a), 1984 Photo Dwight Brooks

including *Le Toit* (5.12a, 1973), *The Flakes* (5.11c, 1973), *The Vampire* (5.11a, 1973), *The Drain Pipe* (5.11b, 1973), *Iron Cross* (5.11b, 1973), *Etude* (5.11a, 1974), *Paisano Overhang* (5.12c, 1973), *Green Arch* (5.11c, 1975), *The Hangover* (5.13a, 1978), and *Stairway to Heaven* (5.12a, 1984).

Chouinard's prophecy of Tahquitz as a proving ground was realized when John Long visited Yosemite, nabbing the first one-day ascent of *The Nose Route* on El Capitan in 1975 with Jim Bridwell and Billy Westbay, and the first free ascent of the East Face of Washington Column (Astroman) with John Bachar and Ron Kauk—two of the most pivotal climbs in American climbing history.

That year (1975) also saw the first free ascent of *The Green Arch* at Tahquitz (5.11c, Rick Accomazzo, John Long, and Tobin Sorenson), and in 1976 Tobin Sorenson made the legendary first ascent of *The Edge* (5.11b R). Tobin wept when his drill bit broke some 40 feet out from his last bolt, but he somehow regained composure to finish drilling, place the bolt, and continue the harrowing lead. John Long led the entire arête of *The Edge* from the very base (called *Turbo Flange,* 5.11c R) in 1984, establishing what is one of the most impressive single pitches on the rock.

It's rarely done because of its terrifying runout—only three protection bolts for the entire 150-foot lead. Falls exceeding 100 feet have been logged on the harrowing *Edge,* one of the most storied free climbs in the United States. Don't pop.

John Bachar's first ascent of *Caliente* (5.12c, 1978) set the bar even higher for pure difficulty, as did Tony Yaniro's first free ascent of the thin crack of *The Pirate* (5.12+), also in 1978.

Darrell Hensel, along with Kevin Powell, kept the ground-up traditional style of the Stonemasters alive through the 1980s and into the 1990s at Suicide Rock, pushing standards even higher with uncompromising style. Kevin and Darrell teamed up for the

Darrell Hensel stance-drilling during the first ascent of *Picante* (5.12a), 1987 Photo Kevin Powell

John Long on the third pitch of *Stairway to Heaven,* during the first free ascent, 1984 Photo Bob Gaines

first free ascent of the first pitch of *Hades* (5.12a, 1980), one of the best hard slab pitches at Suicide, and Darrell's first free ascent of *Ishi* (5.12d, 1985) was a benchmark achievement, as was Darrell's first ascent of *Someone You're Not* (5.13a, 1991).

Bob Gaines leading *The Crucifix* (5.11c), 1995 Photo Sam Roberts

In Chuck Wilt's *Tahquitz and Suicide Rocks* guidebook, which was last published in 1979 and describes 197 routes, Chuck writes: "This may be the last edition of the *Tahquitz and Suicide Guide*. Even climbers of the present generation seem to agree that the basic purpose of the guide has been fulfilled and there is no real need to record more and more difficult variations of existing routes."

Since 1979, however, more that 400 new routes have been climbed, many of which are revered classics. During the last twenty years, a talented group of climbers including Kelly Vaught, Frank Bentwood, Charles Cole, Troy Mayr, Clark Jacobs, Tom Gilge, Scott Erler, Dave Evans, Randy Vogel, Craig Fry, Rob Raker, Todd Gordon, Alan Bartlett, Tony Sartin, Tom Murphy, Erik Roed, John Weinberg, and others have continued to explore and find great new climbs. Kelly Vaught and Frank Bentwood have explored beyond the cliffs of Tahquitz and Suicide, developing entire new areas (such as the Hinterland Wall) on separate cliffs in the Idyllwild area.

I've included first ascent information in this guide to provide a sense of history for the route you're climbing and its place in the evolution of climbing at Tahquitz and Suicide Rocks. Chances are you'll be following in the path of one of the masters of our sport.

Map Legend

 Interstate Highway	Campground
US Highway	Climbing Number
State Highway	Crag/Boulder
Local Road	Cliff Edge
Trail	Mountain Peak
Intermittent Stream	Parking
State/County Park	Restroom
Building/Point of Interest	Town

Topo Legend

o	Belay Stance with Gear or Natural Anchor
x	Bolt
P	Fixed Piton
xx	2– or 3–Bolt Anchor
xx	Rappel Anchor

Kris Solem and Guy Keese on the second pitch of *The Vampire* (5.11a) PHOTO KEVIN POWELL

Tahquitz Rock

Tahquitz Rock is a huge dome-like formation, with its highest cliffs facing northeast, north, northwest, west, and south. To the east, the cliffs of Tahquitz diminish, merging into the surrounding mountainside, forming a notch between the summit area of Tahquitz Rock and the slope of the mountainside leading up to Tahquitz Peak.

As you're looking up at Tahquitz from Humber Park, the Northeast Buttress is the far left section of the rock, and the Northwest Recess is the steep section seen directly above Humber Park. The right side of the rock is the west face, and the south face is around the corner to the right.

Tahquitz Rock Overview

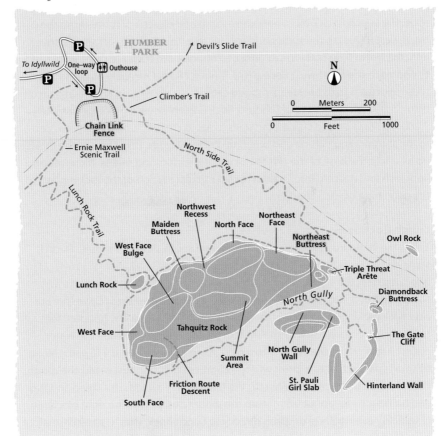

The cliffs are divided into geographical areas, starting at the left side of the rock and moving right. The approaches and descents are described in the area introductions, and the routes are described from left to right (as if you're facing the rock).

Getting there: From the town of Idyllwild, drive uphill (northeast) on either Pine Crest Avenue or North Circle Drive to where they intersect. Turn onto South Circle Drive and make an immediate left onto Fern Valley Road. From this turn, proceed 1.6 miles to Humber Park (GPS: N33 45.901' / W116 41.244'). For the Lunch Rock Trail, park in the first available parking spots. For the North Side Trail, proceed to the upper (one-way) loop of Humber Park. (See Tahquitz and Suicide Rocks Overview map.)

APPROACH TRAILS

There are two approach trails that lead from Humber Park to Tahquitz Rock. For routes from the Maiden Buttress to the South Face (center to right side of the rock), the Lunch Rock Trail is most convenient and direct. For routes from the Northwest Recess to the Hinterland (center to left side of the rock and farther left), the North Side Trail is most direct, although both trails are commonly used to approach the Northwest Recess (see Tahquitz Rock Overview map). Both of these approach trails are steep, rugged climber's trails with an elevation gain of nearly 1,000 feet. The base of Tahquitz Rock is at an elevation of approximately 7,000 feet. Take care to stay on the trails to avoid creating unnecessary erosion to the surrounding hillside and braiding of the main use trail. Once at the rock, a trail traces the base of the cliff to the various sectors and routes. More specific approach and descent information for a particular section of the rock is given at the beginning of each chapter.

Lunch Rock Trail

This is the standard approach for the west and south sides of Tahquitz Rock. It starts on the Ernie Maxwell Trail. The trailhead (GPS: N33 45.889' / W116 41.231') is located near the start of the Humber Park parking area, just before the first sharp bend in the road, 0.2 mile up Fern Valley Road from Forest Drive (the Suicide Rock parking area). Follow the Ernie Maxwell Trail for a few hundred feet to where it crosses a creek (sometimes dry in late season, or when the water district has diverted the water into a pipe), then proceed about 175 yards along this well-graded trail to a point where a climber's trail signpost marks the rough climber's trail that heads straight up the hillside on your left. This steep and rugged trail climbs for about 0.5 mile up the mountainside (staying right of a large talus field), eventually taking you directly to Lunch Rock, which is an informal

Tahquitz Rock Overview

North Gully Wall

Hinterland Wall

West Face
Bulge

The Gate
Cliff
North
Gully

West Face

Diamondback
Buttress

Flintstone
Slab

To
South
Face

North
Buttress

Maiden Buttress

Northeast
Buttress

Northeast Face

Northwest
Recess

Lunch Rock

North Side Trail

Lunch Rock Trail

staging area and gathering spot for climbs on the West Face. Plan on about 30 to 40 minutes for the approach from your car to Lunch Rock. Approaches to specific cliffs are given in the area introductions starting from Lunch Rock. (See Tahquitz and Suicide Rocks Overview map, page vi.)

North Side Trail

This is the best approach for the climbs on the crags east of Tahquitz Rock and Tahquitz Rock's Northeast Face. The approach begins at the start of the Devil's Slide Trail, which is a well-marked and popular hiking trail that begins from the south side of the highest parking area at the top of the Humber Park loop road (GPS: N33 45.874' / W116 41.152'). From the start of the hiking trail, cut immediately to the right and walk just left of a chain-link fence on a trail leading steeply down to a streambed. When you reach the stream (sometimes dry in late season), head left (upstream) for about 100 feet to where a giant log spans the creekbed. Cross the stream, then follow the trail as it climbs steeply out the right side of the drainage. Soon you'll see the great North Face of Tahquitz up and to your right. After about 300 yards from the streambed crossing you'll come to a fork in the trail (GPS: N33 39.369' / W117 50.386'). Take the right fork and continue up the trail as it climbs to Tahquitz Rock and the base of the Northeast Buttress. The first section of rock you'll come to is a small cliff below the main rock with the *Triple Threat Arête* route (GPS: N33 45.710' / W116 40.834'). To get to Diamondback Buttress, The Gate Cliff, St. Pauli Girl Slab, Hinterland Wall, and North Gully Wall, head left. To get to the Northeast Buttress, North Face, Northwest Recess, and Maiden Buttress, head right and follow the trail along the base of the main cliff (see Tahquitz and Suicide Rocks Overview map).

TAHQUITZ DESCENT ROUTES

There are the two commonly used descent routes for Tahquitz Rock: the North Gully (3rd class) and the Friction Route (minimal 4th class). In general, for routes ending on the left side of the rock (Northeast Face to Maiden Buttress) the North Gully is the most convenient descent; for the routes ending on the right side of the rock (West Face Bulge to the South face), the Friction Route is most commonly used. Of the two routes the Friction Route has more difficult route-finding and is slightly more technical and exposed.

North Gully Descent

This is the most convenient descent for routes topping out on the Northeast Face, North Face, and Northwest Recess. The Northeast Face routes finish very

North Gully Overview

near the upper part of the gully, and a short uphill scramble (3rd class) gets you to the start of the gully proper.

For the routes that finish near the summit of Tahquitz Rock, scramble down (3rd class) into a notch between Tahquitz Rock and the hillside above it. Head left (northeast) down the North Gully, which has several 3rd-class sections. Near the base of the gully, head left around the lowest point on the rock, then along a trail back to the base of the Northeast Face.

Friction Route Descent

This 4th-class descent route is most convenient for all routes to the right of the Maiden Buttress, including routes topping out on the West Face Bulge, West Face, and South Face. It's a bit tricky compared to the North Gully descent, so it's advisable to study this description carefully or follow someone who knows the way for your first time down it.

From the vicinity of the summit of Tahquitz Rock, head down and right (west) to where a large boulder sits on the brink of the South Face. From the top of the West Face and South Face climbs (you'll be on the southwest shoulder of the rock), head up low-angle slabs (east) just above the edge of the South Face. Go up and over (or around to the left) a large boulder, down a short chimney/ slot for about 10 feet, then shimmy down a groove for another 10 feet to a

Tahquitz Rock—South Face Overview

Tahquitz Rock—Friction Route Descent Overview

ledge. Move right and down a ramp for about 50 feet, then cut left and head diagonally left across a series of ledges with trees and finally across an open, low-angle slab that leads to the base of the cliff and a trail that contours the South Face, eventually rounding the southwest corner of the rock and leading back to Lunch Rock.

1.

Tahquitz Rock— East Side Crags

The first routes listed here are on completely separate crags to the east of the main Tahquitz Rock. These crags include Owl Rock and Diamondback Buttress. The approaches are listed in the crag descriptions, and all start from the North Side Trail.

OWL ROCK

This is a separate formation located on the hillside to the northeast of Tahquitz's main cliff. It is in the sun most of the day, so the best time to climb here is during cooler weather. Although the approach is a bit arduous, the crag has a nice mix of crack and face climbing, and chances are,

Tahquitz Rock—East Side Crags

if you make the grueling approach, you'll have the crag all to yourself.

Approach: Follow the North Side Trail for several hundred yards from the creek crossing to where it forks (GPS: N33 39.369' / W116 50.386'). Take the left fork and continue for about 200 yards, roughly paralleling the rim of the streambed, until you can see the narrow talus band that extends up to the North Gully. (You'll see the 250-foot-high Diamondback Buttress, with its distinctive summit block, to the left of this talus slope.) Turn left and drop down into the streambed, then turn right and head up the streambed for 150 feet. Cut left and climb back out of the streambed. You'll cross two more streambeds before heading up

a steep slope to Owl Rock. Approach time from Humber Park is approximately 1 hour.

1. The Prey (5.10d) ** **Pitch 1:** Climb a corner/flake up to a roof, move left and over the roof (5.10d) to a bolt, then up to a 2-bolt belay/ rappel anchor at a ledge. **Pitch 2:** (5.10a) Climb a right-facing corner/ flake that arches right, then up a face past three bolts and a fixed pin to the 2-bolt belay/rappel anchor shared with *Bentwood Buttress*. Rappel 80 feet. **Pitch 2 variation** (5.10a): Climb a few feet up the right-facing corner/flake (5.10a), then move left and climb a long crack in a corner (5.7) to a 2-bolt belay/rappel anchor. Descend in two rappels (80 feet, 40

Owl Rock

Owl Rock

feet). **Pro:** 0.25 to 4 inches. **FA:** Kelly Vaught, Kendall Vaught, and Frank Bentwood, September 2003.

2. Bentwood Buttress (5.10b) ** Climb the left side of the arête past seven bolts to a 2-bolt anchor. Rappel 80 feet. **Pro:** 0.25 to 1 inch. **FA:** Frank Bentwood, Kendall Vaught, Kelly Vaught, September 2003.

3. Talon (5.10b) * Climb the arête on the far right side of the formation. 5 bolts to a 2-bolt belay/rappel anchor (60 feet). **FA:** Kelly Vaught and Kendall Vaught, October 2003.

DIAMONDBACK BUTTRESS

This is a separate 250-foot-high formation located immediately to the left of, and at the base of, the North Gully. The climbs feature a mix of slab and face climbing, with a unique summit block.

Approach: Follow the North Side Trail to the start of the North Gully. The Diamondback Buttress is immediately to the left at the beginning of the gully.

1. The Beast (5.11a) ** Lieback/undercling a left-slanting corner (5.10a, 0.4- to 0.75-inch CDs), then climb a slab (5.11a) past six bolts, moving up and right from the last bolt to a ledge with a 2-bolt anchor. (130 feet) The crux is between the fourth and fifth bolts; you can get additional pro (0.4 to 2 inches) between the fifth and sixth bolts. **Pitch 2:** Climb the face on the left past two bolts (5.11a) up to a flake, then past another bolt (5.10a) up to a crack that zigzags, first right, then diagonally back left. Here a sling on a horn protects face climbing up to a ledge below the summit block. **Pitch 3:** A bolt protects bouldery, tricky moves, either traversing left from the bolt (5.11a) or straight up (height-dependent 5.11, a cheatstone can be used). Move left to the

arête; another bolt on the arête's left side protects moves to the top, where you'll find a 2-bolt anchor and a great view. **Descent:** The rappel bolts are a short scramble down the west side of the block (toward Tahquitz Rock). Rappel 100 feet plus some 4th-class downclimbing. **Pro:** to 2 inches. **FA:** Kelly Vaught, Bob Gaines, and Frank Bentwood, August, 2003.

2. Sidewinders (5.10a) * Begin on the right side of the face and climb up to a 5.8 lieback corner that slants left, then up an interesting face past five bolts to a ledge with a 2-bolt anchor. The crux (5.10a) is at the last bolt (130 feet). **Pitch 2:** Climb a 5.9 crack that arches right (or the easier face just to the right), lieback an unprotected (5.7 R) right-facing corner, then squirm up an awkward (5.10a) off-width. Belay at the base of the summit block. **Pitch 3:** Go around the right (west) side of the block, ascending an easy face on jugs to a belay at a notch. There is a 2-bolt anchor at the summit. **Descent:** The rappel bolts are a short scramble down the west side of the block (toward Tahquitz Rock). Rappel 100 feet plus some 4th-class downclimbing. **Pro:** to 3 inches. **FA:** Bob Gaines, Kelly Vaught, and Frank Bentwood, August 2003.

Diamondback Buttress

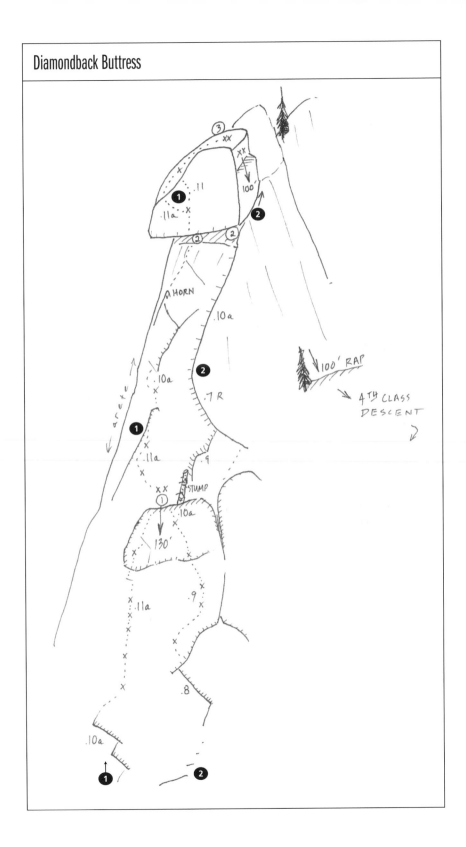

2.

The Hinterland

This area of steep cliffs sits in a rock amphitheater up and left (east) of the North Gully. The main cliff, called the Hinterland Wall, has an assortment of good crack climbs, in addition to some fun face climbs. Most of the routes that have been done are included here, and will give you plenty to do if you decide to spend a day here. The area is somewhat secluded and offers a view of both Tahquitz and Suicide Rocks. It gets shade in the early morning.

Approach: Take the North Side Trail up to the first cliffs of Tahquitz. Head left into the broad base of the North Gully, following the trail a short distance up the North Gully and onto talus. As you ascend the gully, The Gate Cliff is to your left and the St. Pauli Girl Slab is farther up the gully, directly ahead. The gully splits, with the North Gully on the right and another gully leading up and left

from the St. Pauli Girl Slab to the Hinterland Wall.

Descent: All routes have single-rope (100-foot) rappel descent routes.

THE GATE CLIFF

This is the tiny cliff on the left side of the main North Gully, before you get to St. Pauli Girl Slab. It gets shade in the early morning.

1. The Gate (5.10a) Jam a crack in a corner up to a 2-bolt belay/rappel anchor. **Pro:** 0.5 to 4 inches. **FA:** Kelly Vaught, Kendall Vaught, and Frank Bentwood, August 2002.

2. Gerber Baby (5.11b) * Climb a short left-facing corner to a sweet arête with two bolts. 2-bolt belay/rappel anchor. **Pro:** 0.25 to 1 inch. **FA:** Kelly Vaught, Kendall Vaught, and Frank Bentwood, August 2002.

ST. PAULI GIRL SLAB

This fine little friction slab is located in the center of the North Gully where the gully splits, with the North Gully descent route to the right and the gully leading up to Hinterland Wall on the left. It is in the shade most of the day during the summer.

1. St. Pauli Girl (5.11b) * Weave past some little bulges, then snake your way up the slab past four bolts to a 2-bolt anchor (100 feet). **Pro:** thin to 1 inch. **FA:** Unknown.

2. Smears for Fears (5.11a) * Climb flakes up to friction past six bolts on the very right side of the slab to a 2-bolt anchor (100 feet). **Pro:** thin to 0.75 inch. **FA:** Frank Bentwood, Kelly Vaught, Kendall Vaught, and Zach Romero, August 2002.

3. Woman Up (5.8) Lieback the clean right-facing corner, climb over overlaps, then up a slab to the communal 2-bolt anchor (60 feet). **Pro:** to 2 inches. **FA:** Kelly Vaught, Frank Bentwood, and Kendell Vaught, October 2009.

4. Man Up (5.10b R) Climb a beautiful 3-bolt slab, then climb easily over overlaps up to a 2-bolt anchor (60 feet). Getting to the first bolt is a bit scary (5.10a R). From the first bolt, go right then up and left to the second bolt. Climb just left of the second bolt, then back right to the third bolt. **Pro:** to 2 inches. **FA:** Kelly Vaught and Frank Bentwood, October 2009.

5. Chin Up (5.9) Climb up to a bolt, move right, then back left to a flake. Climb past overlaps and up a slab to a 2-bolt belay/rappel anchor (60 feet). **Pro:** to 3 inches. **FA:** Kelly Vaught and Frank Bentwood, October 2009.

St. Pauli Girl Slab—Center

St. Pauli Girl Slab—Right Side

6. Maneater (5.10b) * Undercling, reach, and mantle around the corner, then climb a delicate slab. 4 bolts to a 2-bolt anchor (60 feet). **FA:** Frank Bentwood and Kelly Vaught, October 2009.

HINTERLAND WALL

The Hinterland Wall is located several hundred yards up the gully left of St. Pauli Girl Slab. This is the main attraction of the area, with a high concentration of crack climbs, including the classic *Hinterland Crack* (5.11b), and a few excellent face routes. The main cliff is in the shade in the morning.

1. Goose Step (5.10d) Climb past a bolt to right-slanting thin cracks to a 2-bolt belay/rappel anchor. **Pro:** thin to 2 inches. **FA:** Frank Bentwood and Russ Romero, 2003.

2. Fatherland (5.10a) Climb a thin flake system up to the 2-bolt anchor. **Pro:** small to 2 inches. **FA:** Frank Bentwood and Russ Romero, 2003.

3. When Fools Rush In (5.10c) * Climb a crack that forks—take the left branch up past a fixed pin and bolt, then climb up and left to the 2-bolt anchor. **Pro:** small to 2 inches. **FA:** Frank Bentwood and Russ Romero, 2003.

4. Fraulein (5.10a) Jam the crack on the upper tier that diagonals up and

Hinterland Wall

right to the 2-bolt anchor shared with *Hinterland Crack*. **Pro:** to 3 inches. **FA:** Alison Tudor, Kelly Vaught, and Frank Bentwood, August 2006.

5. Hinterland Crack (5.11b) ******
Perhaps the best route on the wall. **Pitch 1:** Start as for *When Fools Rush In,* then take the right branch of the crack all the way right to another vertical crack; jam this (5.9) up to a ledge with a 2-bolt belay/rappel anchor below a steep corner (100 feet). **Pitch 2:** Climb the right-facing corner up to a little roof, then turn it on the left and climb a steep crack (5.11b) past two bolts to the top and a 2-bolt belay/rappel anchor (90 feet). **Pro:** to 3.5 inches. **FA:** Unknown.

6. Lederhosen (5.10a) ***Pitch 1:**
Climb the left of two cracks (5.8), moving right to the right-hand crack near the top up to the 2-bolt anchor shared with *Hinterland Crack*. **Pitch 2:** (5.10a) Climb a long crack to the top. Rappel *Hinterland Crack*. **Pro:** to 3 inches. **FA:** Kelley Vaught and Frank Bentwood, July 2004.

7. Community Property (5.7) This is the left-facing dihedral system that ends at the ledge and 2-bolt anchor shared with *He Said She Said*. **Descent:** Two 100-foot rappels. **Pro:** to 3 inches. **FA:** Bob Gaines, Frank Bentwood, and Kelly Vaught, August 2003.

8. He Said She Said (5.10b) * Climb cracks up to the right side of a bulge, then move left, over the bulge up to a bolt on the face. Follow cracks up and left to the arête, then climb past three bolts (5.10b) up to a nice ledge and a 2-bolt anchor. **Descent:** Rappel 100 feet to a bolt anchor, then make a second 100-foot rappel to the base. **Pro:** CDs from 0.3 to 3 inches. **FA:** Bob Gaines, Frank Bentwood, and Kelly Vaught, August 2003.

9. Octoberfest (5.11a) ** This steep pitch powers through the overhangs on the right side of the cliff. Climb past two fixed pins, then weave through the roofs past four bolts to a 2-bolt anchor. **Pro:** to 2 inches. **FA:** Frank Bentwood and Kelly Vaught, July 2004.

NORTH GULLY WALL

This 300-foot-high cliff is located on the left side of the upper North Gully, just below the top of the gully. Approach is via the North Gully. It is in the shade most of the day. If you don't mind dealing with a bit of lichen, this cliff offers summer shade and a good escape from the weekend crowds on the main cliff.

1. Mercy of the Sisters (5.8+) * This route starts on the left side of the cliff. Begin by traversing 3rd class ledges up and left to the base of a crack system. **Pitch 1:** (170 feet) Climb up a corner and over a bulge to a small right-facing corner that fades to a seam, then up past a flake (5.8+). Continue up the crack past a small roof. Belay at the base of a big right-slanting corner at a

Hinterland Wall—Right Side

mountain mahogany (semi-hanging). **Pitch 2:** Work up the corner and over an overhang (5.7), then traverse right to a gully. Move up the gully, passing a small roof (5.6). Belay a bit higher. **Descent:** Up and right (3rd class) to the summit ridge. Scramble down the left (south) side of the blocky ridge (3rd class), then head back down the North Gully. **Pro:** to 3 inches. **FA:** Christian Burrell and Brian "Gonzo" Gonzales, June 1999.

2. Dirty Girl (5.10b) * This route is located in the center of the wall. As the name suggests, it's a bit lichenous, but will only improve with traffic. **Pitch 1:** Climb a slab up to the steeper section where a bolt protects moves over a small roof (5.10b), with a pin just a bit higher. Follow flakes, exiting left to a 2-bolt anchor. **Pitch 2:** Head up and right past four bolts to a roof and move left to another 2-bolt anchor. **Descent:** Rappel the route in two 100-foot rappels. **Pro:** small to 2 inches. **FA:** Kelly Vaught, Kendall Vaught, and Frank Bentwood, September 2007.

3. East Crack (5.10a) ** This fine finger crack hasn't seen much action due to its obscure location, but it deserves more attention. Begin on the right side of the face and follow the thin crack up to a 2-bolt anchor (100-foot rappel). **Pro:** to 2 inches. **FA:** Unknown.

North Gully Wall

Andrea Konig leads *Y Crack*
(5.10b) Photo Kevin Powell

3.

Tahquitz Rock—Northeast Face

When you look up from Humber Park, the Northeast Face of Tahquitz can be seen as the far left side of the rock. This face is characterized by long, less than vertical dihedrals and cracks that extend for hundreds of feet up the rock, in addition to a myriad of flakes from exfoliating slabs. On the faces between the dihedrals are some very fine face climbs that combine thin features and smooth friction slabs.

The far left side of the face forms a buttress, called the Northeast Buttress. At the base of the Northeast Buttress are two small, separate outcrops where Triple Threat Arête and Y Crack Buttress are located.

In the center of the face, the *Northeast Face East* and *Northeast Face West* routes follow fairly obvious right-facing dihedrals that extend for hundreds of feet up the rock, forming

Northeast Face Routes

a rough triangle near the center of the face and joining at the top of the triangle. These routes serve as good reference points to find the starts of some of the other climbs.

Approach: The North Side Trail
Descent: The North Gully

TRIPLE THREAT ARÊTE

1. Triple Threat Arête (5.11b) * This route is located on a small pillar on the very lowest section of the Northeast Buttress, just a few feet left of where the North Side Trail first meets the base of Tahquitz Rock. Climb the left side of the arête, passing several small roofs, moving left near the top to surmount the largest roof. 5 bolts to a 2-bolt anchor. **Descent:** Rappel 80 feet. **Pro:** 0.5 to 2 inches. **FA:** Kelly Vaught, Kendall Vaught, and Frank Bentwood, August 2004. The route just to the left is called *P90X* (5.10d), 5 bolts to a 2-bolt anchor.

Triple Threat Arête

Y CRACK BUTTRESS

This small rampart is a separate buttress, located on the far left side of the Northeast Face, easily identified as a short, steep, green face, split by a beautiful hand crack.

Approach: From where the North Side Trail first meets Tahquitz Rock, head right a short distance; the Y Crack Buttress is seen directly above you. A short, easy 5th-class pitch up a corner/gully that diagonals right to left is required to get to the base of the cracks.

Descent: From the top of the Y Crack Buttress, a 100-foot rappel from bolts gets you to the base of the cracks. From here you can make another rappel (100 feet) from a tree to the ground.

1. Y Crack (5.10b) ** Excellent, sustained jamming up a very steep wall. The start of the crack has two branches (both about 5.9) that merge a short way up; the crux is just above where they join. **Pro:** to 3 inches, including several extra CDs in the 1.5- to 2.5-inch range. **FA:** Jim Wilson, et al., 1975.

Y Crack Buttress

NORTHEAST FACE—LEFT SIDE

Approach: From where the North Side Trail first meets Tahquitz Rock, head up and right for about 200 feet to the base of the main cliff. *El Whampo* and *El Grandote* are located a short distance up and left, up a gully. A prominent, 5-foot diameter pine tree (sugar pine) marks the start of the gully.

1. El Whampo (5.7) ** Although the upper pitches are a bit chossy, the second pitch is perhaps the best 5.7 jam crack on the cliff. Start down and right from a huge right-facing dihedral that extends several hundred feet up the cliff, eventually slanting right to form a series of overhanging flakes. Climb a gully (4th class) up and left to the start of the harder climbing. **Pitch 1:** (5.5) Climb up cracks to the giant dihedral, then up over several overlaps in the corner to a belay level with some tiny scrub oak trees. **Pitch 2:** (130 feet) Climb about 10 feet above the belay, then traverse right across a white slab on pure friction (5.4 PG) over to the crack. Jam the classic, straight-in crack, which begins with hand jams and thins to fingers (5.7). At the top, traverse down and right and belay on a blocky ledge. **Pitch 3, left variation:** Up a flake system (passing a 2-bolt anchor) to the overhangs, moving right to belay beneath a break in the roofs. **Pitch 3, right variation:** Up the flakes for about 20 feet, then step right onto a friction slab with a thin seam that

Northeast Face Routes

diagonals up and right (5.7 PG/R). Continue up to the belay beneath the break in the roofs. **Pitch 4:** Climb through the overhang (5.7) and up a shallow trough, then lieback a flake that arches right (5.7) into a series of overlapping flakes, belaying partway up the arch at a semi-hanging belay. (Easier pitches are possible farther left above the overhang.) **Pitch 4/5:** From the belay under the overhangs, climb diagonally right, under the overhangs for about 50 feet, then cross the overhangs at a weakness and belay a bit higher at a tree. Climb flakes up and left to the ledge with the stout pine tree belay. **Pitch 5:** (5.5) Up easier cracks and slab to a belay on a large ledge at a squat pine tree with a 3-foot diameter trunk. **Pitch**

6: A 4th-class pitch up a gully leads up and left to the top. **Direct start:** For a great direct start, climb the first two pitches of El Grandote (5.9), then traverse left across an easy ledge that leads to the dihedral on El Whampo's first pitch. **Pro:** thin to 3 inches. **FA:** Roy Coats, Larry Reynolds, Russ McLean, and D. Ross, 1964.

2. El Grandote (5.9) ** The start of this route can be identified by a prominent right-facing dihedral capped by a 10-foot roof, on the far left side of the Northeast Face where a gully leads up and left. **Pitch 1:** (130 feet, 5.9) Rope up in the gully where it first becomes steep and climb into the dihedral until about 30 feet below the roof, then up wild moves through cracks out the

El Whampo/El Grandote

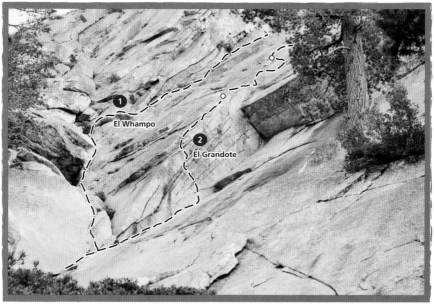

left wall of the dihedral to the arête (a bit loose). Follow a thin flake just left of the arête to a nice belay ledge just a few feet above the level of the roof. **Pitch 2:** (40 feet, 5.8) Up and right to a thin seam, then face climb just left of the seam, moving back right to a slim right-facing corner and up to a long ledge. Move left about 20 feet and belay at the base of a 20-foot-high right-facing corner. Pitches 1 and 2 can be combined, but you'll get rope drag for the delicate face climbing on pitch 2. **Pitch 3:** Climb the right-facing corner and step right across the face to another corner. After about 15 feet up the corner, move right again to a beautiful, thin lieback flake and follow it up to beneath overhangs. Traverse right under the roofs until below an obvious break, and belay here. **Pitch 4:** Climb overlapping flakes up through the weakness in the overhangs to a belay at a blocky ledge shared with *El Whampo*. **Pitches 5–8:** See the *El Whampo* description for the finish. **Pro:** thin to 3 inches. **FA:** Yvon Chouinard and Harry Daley, May 1961. **FFA:** Bob Kamps and TM Herbert, 1963.

3. El Monte (5.10b R) ** Interesting, varied, but runout slab climbing that connects various cracks and flakes with some routefinding challenges. To enjoy this route, you should be solid leading 5.10 face. Begin at the base of *Northeast Face East*. **Pitch 1:** Climb a 4th-class pitch up to ledges at the start of the more difficult climbing.

Pitch 2: Move up and right, then up and left, following a thin flake system. Traverse left onto the face, then climb up a smooth section past two bolts (5.10b) to a lieback flake (2- to 3-inch pro), followed by a few face moves (5.9) up to a semi-hanging two-bolt belay (100-foot rappel from here to the ground). Two 3-inch CDs are useful for this pitch. **Pitch 3:** Begin with intimidating climbing up a left-leaning thin crack (with a bolt) to a little corner. Head up and right on knobbier face climbing to a crack that leans left. Belay at a ledge with a 2-bolt anchor. **Pitch 4:** Place a nut in a tiny corner and move right (5.10-) past a curiously located bolt (hard to see from below), then traverse right (5.9, scary) to a crack. Follow the crack until it peters out, then climb the slab up to a bolt (5.10a). Continue with thin slab moves (5.10b) up to another bolt, then traverse right and climb a thin crack (5.9) to a 2-bolt belay. **Pitch 4 direct variation:** (5.10c R) At the first bolt, climb straight up a small left-facing corner (no pro), then traverse up and left (5.10c R) to a bolt. Continue straight up to another bolt, then traverse right to join the normal route at its second bolt. **Descent:** The best descent is to make three rappels with two 60-meter ropes: (1) Rappel diagonally to the right about 60 feet to the 2-bolt anchor at the top of *Grace Slick*'s second pitch. (2) Rappel 110 feet to 2-bolt anchor at the top of *Grace Slick*'s first pitch. (3) Rappel 200

Northeast Face Slabs

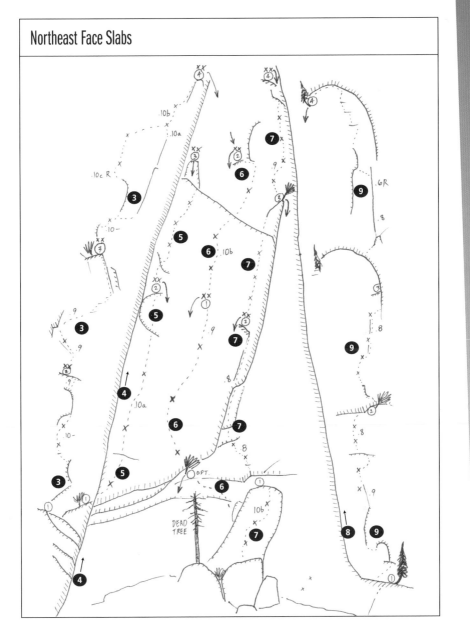

feet to the ground. **Pro:** to 3 inches, including thin nuts and TCUs plus two 3-inch CDs. **FA:** Fred Zeil, et al., 1979. **FA, direct variation pitch 3:** Dave Evans and Rob Raker, 1987.

4. Northeast Face East (5.6) Listed here for a point of reference, this climb ascends the left of the two most prominent and unbroken right-facing dihedrals that extend several hundred feet up the Northeast Face. The start is found near the bottom of the gully that leads up and left to *El Grandote* and *El Whampo,* near a huge, 5-foot diameter pine tree (sugar pine). You'll also see a large, dead pine tree up a ways on the right side. The dihedral starts as a right-facing corner, changes into a left-facing dihedral, then is right-facing for hundreds of feet. It eventually merges with the dihedral of *Northeast Face West.* In between these two dihedrals are the slab routes *Partners in Crime, Grace Slick,* and *Coup de Grace.* **Pro:** to 2 inches. **FA:** Don Wilson and Royal Robbins, September 1954.

5. Partners in Crime (5.10a PG) * This slab route climbs the face just right of the *Northeast Face East* dihedral, on the left side of the *Grace Slick* slab. **Pitch 1:** Climb a short, easy (5.0) pitch up to a belay ledge level with the roof below the *Grace Slick* slab. **Pitch 2:** Move right to the first bolt. Climb past two more bolts (5.10a), plus some gear placements, up to a 2-bolt anchor. **Pitch 3:** Continue up the slab (5.10a), passing three more bolts, to another 2-bolt anchor. **Descent:** Rappel the route with two ropes. **Pro:** medium nuts and CDs to 3 inches. **FA:** Mark Uphus and Bill Kramer, October 2003.

6. Grace Slick (5.10b PG) ** A superb slab climb up some very smooth rock. Begin right of *Northeast Face East* and just right of a huge dead pine tree.

Pitch 1: Climb up to a massive mountain mahogany (optional belay here) beneath a right-slanting overhang. Go over the roof, then friction past three bolts (5.9) up to a 2-bolt anchor. **Pitch 2:** Smear past three bolts (5.10b) up to another 2-bolt anchor. **Descent:** Rappel the route with two ropes. **Pro:** to 3 inches. **FA:** Jim Wilson, Peter Wilkening, and Chris Wegener, 1975.

7. Coup de Grace (5.10b PG) * This fun, four-pitch route climbs up to and then along the right side of the *Grace Slick* slab. Begin slightly down and right from *Grace Slick* at a separate, triangular-shaped slab. **Pitch 1:** (5.10b) Climb the slab past three bolts to a belay at a notch. **Pitch 2:** (5.8) Work over the roof, then up and left past two bolts to a right-facing flake system. Go over a roof in the flakes, then up to a 2-bolt belay stance on the slab. **Pitch 3:** (5.9) Slab climbing past three bolts leads to a ledge. Climb up and right from here to a belay at a tree. **Pitch 4:** (5.9) Follow the right edge of the slab past four bolts up to a 2-bolt anchor. **Descent:** Rappel the route with two ropes. **Pro:** to 3 inches. **FA:** Bill Cramer and Mark Uphus, August 2004.

8. Northeast Face West (5.7) * This is the most prominent right-facing corner near the center of the North Face, identified as a 5-foot-high dihedral that extends several hundred feet up the face. This dihedral merges with the dihedral of *Northeast Face East* after several pitches. The route is sustained, and most of the belays are from small stances. Toward the top the climbing deteriorates somewhat, and there are many ways to go. Begin with a short 5.1 pitch up onto a ledge with a huge, 4-foot diameter pine tree (sugar pine). From here, follow the right-facing dihedral to where it merges with *Northeast Face East*. Continue up the dihedral system until it fades into blocky overhangs, then follow the crack through the overhangs (5.7). Above the overhangs the crack branches into three distinct forks, the right crack being the easiest variation. Any of the three cracks lead to the stout pine tree belay at a big ledge shared with *El Whampo,* where a 4th-class pitch up and left takes you to the top. **Pro:** thin to 3 inches. **FA:** Chuck and Ellen Wilts, 1955.

9. Too Biased (5.9 PG) * An interesting slab climb that will test your routefinding and anchoring skills. The less than perfect rock and some long runouts add to the excitement, as does the rappel descent that uses some fairly tiny trees. Begin just right of and below the right-facing dihedral of *Northeast Face West*. **Pitch 1:** (5.1) Climb a short (30 feet) cliff up to a large ledge with a 4-foot diameter pine tree (sugar pine). **Pitch 2:** (130 feet) Climb up to a small arch, then left to a thin flake that peters out into a thin seam. Follow this up to a bolt (5.9), then climb the slab past three more bolts up to a roof (3-inch CD). Undercling right to a

hanging belay at a fixed pin and rickety bush (can be backed up with 0.4- to 0.5-inch and 3.5-inch CDs). **Pitch 3:** Climb the overhang by standing on the bush, then follow a thin flake up to a slab with bolts. Climb up and right (5.8) past three bolts to a seam; above the fourth bolt, move right into a right-facing dihedral. Belay a short distance up this at a tiny stance (2-inch CDs). **Pitch 4:** Continue up the corner, exiting right and up a small stance. Follow a thin seam in a groove (5.8) with sparse pro (thin nuts, small TCUs)—the upper section is largely unprotected (5.6 R). When the seam peters out, move left to a thin flake and lieback up this for about 15 feet, then continue with runout but easier slab moves up to an arch (3-inch CD). Traverse down and left along the arch for about 20 feet, with some very awkward moves getting around tree branches, to a hanging belay at a pine tree. **Descent:** The easiest descent is to rappel with two ropes. With one 60-meter rope you can descend in four rappels: (1) Rappel 100 feet to a small mountain mahogany (and solid rock spike) on the left side of the *Northeast Face West* corner. (2) Rappel to the bolt belay of *Coup de Grace.* (3) Rappel to the huge mountain mahogany on *Grace Slick.* (4) Rappel to the ground. **Pro:** thin to medium nuts, TCUs, and CDs to 3.5 inches. Include several 0.4 to 1 inch and several 1 to 2.5 inches, plus one 3 inches and one 4 inches. **FA:** Tom Beck and Mike McCoy, August 1993.

Northwest Recess Face Routes Topo

4

Northwest Recess

The Northwest Recess is the sector of Tahquitz Rock bordered by the North Buttress on the left and the Maiden Buttress on the right. This section of the cliff is noticeably steeper than the Northeast Face, with a vertical rise of about 800 feet, and contains an assortment of Tahquitz's very best moderate multi-pitch climbs, including *The Long Climb* (5.8) and *Whodunit* (5.9). *Whodunit* can be identified as the very prominent right-facing dihedral extending for almost the entire length of the cliff. The cliff is in the shade most of the morning during the summer months and gets sun in the afternoon.

Approach: The approach to the Northwest Recess is commonly made from either the North Side Trail or the Lunch Rock Trail.

From the Lunch Rock Trail: From Lunch Rock, walk left and slightly down along the "toe" of the Maiden Buttress, then scramble up over a notch. The Northwest Recess is a few hundred feet uphill to your right.

From the North Side Trail: Where the North Side Trail first reaches the base of the cliff, walk right along the base of the Northeast Face, then a few hundred feet uphill and to the right of the North Buttress to reach the Northwest Recess.

Descent: Descent can be made by using either the Friction Route or the North Gully—it takes roughly the same amount of time to descend either route and return to the base.

1. The Souvenir (5.10d) * This is a long route, with a good mix of roof, slab, and crack climbing. Begin just right of the indistinct North Buttress, on the left side of the Northwest Recess. **Pitch 1:** Climb an easy crack system (5.2) to a good ledge about 40 feet below roofs. **Pitch 2:** Climb directly through the center of the roofs (5.10c), or climb through the roofs on the left side (5.8). Belay about 40 feet higher at a large pine tree. Move the belay to the far right of the ledge. **Pitch 3:** (165 feet) Make a fingertip traverse up and right to the dogleg crack on *Sahara Terror,* then climb straight up a thin crack to a fixed pin (5.9) and onto a beautiful slab (with intermittent thin cracks and flakes) past six bolts to a belay stance beneath a small overhang with a mountain mahogany. At the fourth bolt you can go up and left (5.10d), or take a slightly easier route (5.10b/c)

Souvenir and Sahara Terror

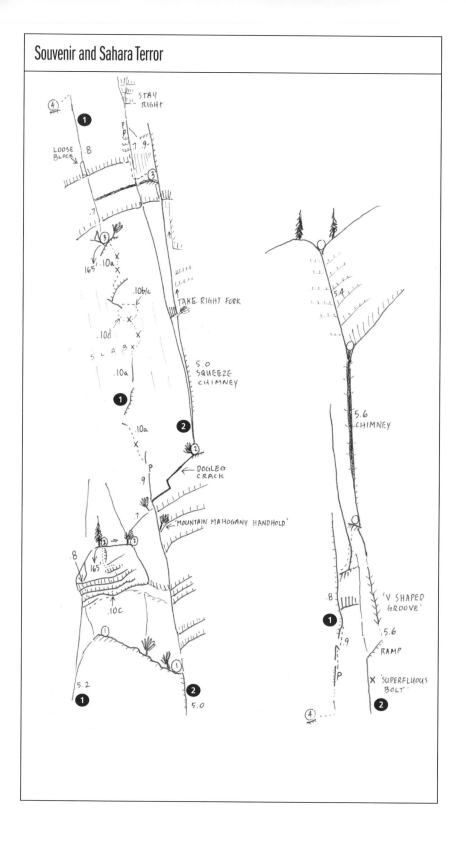

by moving up and slightly right of the bolt, then traversing left. You can make a rappel descent from here with two ropes (two 165-foot rappels). **Pitch 4:** Climb 60 feet up a vertical crack (5.8), taking care as you pass a loose chockstone at the second overhang, and belay at an area of shattered rock on the left. The most solid crack for anchoring is slightly down and left (2- to 3-inch CDs). **Pitch 5:** Move right, then climb up a steep corner (5.9), over a small roof, and up to a belay shared with *Sahara Terror*. **Pitch 6:** Up a deep chimney (5.6). **Pitch 7:** A 5.4 crack system leads up and left to the top. **Pro:** medium nuts, two each CDs to 3.5 inches. **FA:** Bob Gaines and Charlie Peterson, August 1995.

2. Sahara Terror (5.7) ** A long, moderate route with great variety. **Pitch 1:** Climb an easy (5.0) pitch up to a belay with a mountain mahogany (100 feet). **Pitch 2:** Climb a right-facing corner over a series of tiny overlaps, then surmount an overhang via a mountain mahogany handhold. Continue up to a prominent 8-inch-wide dogleg crack and follow this right to a belay at the main corner at a stance with a small mountain mahogany (170 feet). **Pitch 3:** Squirm up a squeeze chimney (5.0) until the crack forks; take the right fork and follow this crack until you reach the base of a steeper headwall. Belay here at a stance with a horizontal crack (0.5- to 2.5-inch CDs). At this juncture many climbers have reported difficult routefinding,

Northwest Recess—Left Side

as there are several ways to go. **Pitch 4:** Step down and left for 6 feet, then climb a left-facing corner over several small overlaps for about 20 feet (5.7) up to two closely spaced fixed pins. Follow the crack system for about 50 feet up to a superfluous bolt. Continue 15 feet up the crack, then traverse right for 10 feet on an easy ramp to a 5.6 move that leads to a V-shaped groove; belay about 30 feet higher at a ledge. **Pitch 4, right variation:** (5.9-) Lieback a 1-inch crack in a steep left-facing corner up to a roof, then step down and left around the roof and traverse 10 feet left to join the normal route. **Pitch 5:** Climb easy (4th class) terrain for 40 feet, then up a 5.6 chimney (from this point onward the route follows this same crack system). **Pitch 6:** Follow the crack system (5.4) to the top. **Pro:** to 3 inches. **FA:** William Shand, Roy Gorin, and Paul Flinchbaugh, July 1942. **FFA:** Bill Pabst and Spencer Austin, 1954.

3. Edgehogs (5.10d) ** This route ascends the long and prominent arête on the left side of the *Whodunit* dihedral. Seen from the parking lot at Humber Park, this arête is highlighted in the afternoon sun. **Pitch 1:** Begin just left of *Whodunit* and climb flakes up to a blank slab section with a bolt and a piton that protect slab climbing (5.10a) up to the 3-bolt belay shared with *Whodunit*. **Pitch 2:** (5.10d) Spectacular face climbing up the great arête leads past ten bolts to a tiny

stance with a 2-bolt anchor. You can place some thin gear between the first and second bolt. **Pitch 3:** Slap and smear up the rounded arête past three bolts (5.10c) to another 2-bolt stance at a bush (1-inch CD for pro above the third bolt). At the third bolt you can also move around the corner to the right, then back left to the arête for an easier variation (5.10a/b). **Pitch 4:** Climb to a bolt at a small roof, move right and climb a thin right-facing flake, moving left onto face climbing, then climb directly up to a roof. Step left over the lip (5.10a) to a bolt. Climb right past another bolt to the arête (5.10b), then continue up a thin flake system (medium nuts, CDs from 0.4 to 1.5 inches) to a 2-bolt belay. You can rappel the route from here with two ropes (four rappels). **Pitch 5:** Climb 40 feet of easy ground, then stay right and climb flakes on the edge of the arête (stay very close to *Whodunit*) up to a belay stance at a fixed pin. **Pitch 6:** Climb the crack directly above the belay, moving right to the arête, then climb an easier (5.4 R) but unprotected slab up to and over two small roofs (again staying close to *Whodunit*) onto a slab and up (5.8) to a bolt. Belay about 40 feet higher beneath the big overhang. **Pitch 7:** Surmount the roof at a fixed pin and bolt (5.10c), then climb up and right to a belay shared with *Whodunit*. **Pitch 8:** (5.0) Climb the last pitch of *Whodunit* to the top. **Pro:** thin to 3 inches. **FA, pitches 1 and 2:**

Bob Gaines and Clark Jacobs, August 1992. **FA, pitches 3 and 4:** Bob Gaines, Todd Gordon, and Bob Austin, July 1997. **FA, pitches 5, 6, 7:** Bob Gaines and Charlie Peterson, August 1998.

4. The Incision (5.11b) *
From the bolted first belay on *Edgehogs/Whodunit,* climb up to *Edgehogs's* first bolt, traverse left to a tiny corner, then up to a second bolt. Face climb (5.11a) up to a small roof. Continue up a slab past three more bolts, up over another little roof, then follow a very thin, offset crack (5.11b) past a fixed pin and a bolt up to a 2-bolt anchor. **Descent:** Make two rappels back down the route with two ropes (165 feet). **Pro:** thin to 2 inches. **FA:** Bob Gaines and Clark Jacobs, 1992.

5. Whodunit (5.9) *** A Tahquitz top ten and a must-do for the grade. If you look up from Humber Park in late-afternoon light, the route can easily be seen as the long right-facing, sunlit dihedral extending nearly the entire length up the Northwest Recess. **Pitch 1:** Begin at the base of the Northwest Recess and climb up and

Northwest Recess—Edgehogs/Whodunit, Lower Pitches

Northwest Recess—
Edgehogs/Whodunit,
Upper Pitches

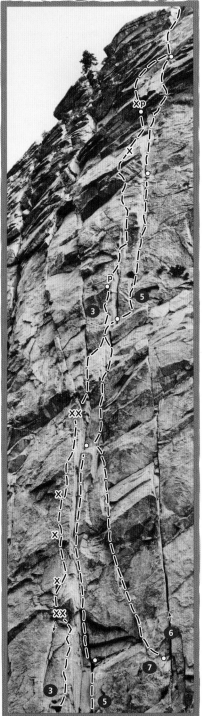

left to a right-facing flake system. Follow this until it becomes progressively more difficult and leads to the crux—the crack thins and goes over a small overlap (5.9, thin nuts or TCUs required)—then traverse up and left past an arch to a 3-bolt belay stance at the base of the main right-facing dihedral (150 feet). **Pitch 2:** Stem and lieback the right-facing dihedral (5.7) to a series of ledges with bushes; belay at the highest ledge with a bush (110 feet). **Pitch 3:** Climb a face move (5.8) past a flake to the crack on the right, then jam the crack in the left-facing corner to a belay stance at the base of a chimney (95 feet). (You can also extend this pitch and belay at a small ledge about 30 feet above the exit from the chimney.) **Pitch 4:** Climb the intimidating "bombay" chimney, exiting out the top via some tricky jams (5.9). Continue jamming the crack past a mountain mahogany up to a belay at a nice ledge (150 feet) (0.3- to 1-inch gear). **Pitch 5:** Climb the crack on the right past a chockstone. Higher, where the crack widens, move left to avoid the off-width crack and climb a flake on the left side of the dihedral, moving back right to the main corner and up to a ledge with a tree stump (100 feet). **Pitch 6:** Climb the right of two cracks (which becomes the main corner) to a belay at a tiny sloping stance at blocks about 40 feet below overhangs. **Pitch 7:** Climb the crack to just below the overhangs, move right under the roofs via face climbing (5.7) for about 30 feet, then power through a weakness in the overhangs (5.8) and up to a belay at a tree at a low-angle left-facing dihedral. **Pitch 8:** Continue up the corner and over an easy (5.4) overhang to 4th-class climbing to the top. Pitches 7 and 8 can be combined for one long final pitch. **Pro:** to 3 inches, including three each CDs from 1 to 3 inches. **FA:** (5.8, A1) Royal Robbins and Joe Fitschen, September 1957. **FFA:** Tom Higgins and Bob Kamps, 1966.

6. The Swallow Direct (5.10a) *
Pitch 3 is one of the classic squeeze chimneys on Tahquitz. Start about 40 feet right of *Whodunit* in a broken left-facing corner system on the right side of a rock apron that leads upward to a steeper headwall. **Pitch 1:** Climb a long pitch up to a belay at two fixed pins. **Pitch 2:** Continue up to where the rock steepens and presents two crack options: Jam the crack on the left (5.10a) that leads straight up to a belay at the base of a deep crack. The original route traversed far to the left to avoid this crack, then traversed back right (that detour is the route *The Gulp*). **Pitch 3:** Squirm your way (5.9-) up the strenuous crack (heel-toe jams help). A fixed pin and slung chockstone can be used for pro, along with a large (3-inch) camming device. Belay just before the crack steepens, at a sloping ledge. **Pitch 4:** Lieback/jam the thin crack through a bulge (5.10a) up to a broad ledge system

that extends across the Northwest Recess. Traverse left to finish via *Whodunit* or move right and finish up *Consolation Direct*. **Pro:** to 4 inches. **FA:** Chuck Wilts and Royal Robbins, June 1952.

7. The Gulp (5.9) * From the base of the squeeze chimney on *The Swallow,* this variation climbs the crack that diagonals up and left to intersect *Whodunit*. **Pro:** to 3 inches, including several from 2 to 3 inches. **FA:** P. Gerhard and D. Ross, 1965.

8. Constellation (5.12a) ** The first two pitches make an excellent direct start to *Consolation*. Pitches 3 and 4 offer gorgeous slab climbing in a stunning location. Begin at the very lowest point on the narrow slab between *The Swallow* and *Consolation*. **Pitch 1:** Climb the center of the slab (5.8), belaying at a blocky ledge on the left block on the highest ledge (165 feet). **Pitch 2:** (5.10b) Climb up to a bolt, then traverse left and climb a left-facing corner to a belay ledge. (From here you can climb up a short distance, then traverse right to join *Consolation*.) **Pitch 3:** (5 bolts) Up and over a series of overlaps, then make a tenuous traverse left (5.11c) to a 2-bolt belay. **Pitch 4:** (3 bolts) A short, smooth slab pitch with a showstopper crux above the third bolt (5.12a) leads up to another 2-bolt anchor. Another pitch (5.11d R) has been done, but I really can't recommend it

Constellation

due to a loose rock feature that can't be bypassed. **Descent:** Rappel the route with two ropes (165-foot rappels), the last rappel from a mountain mahogany. **Pro:** to 2 inches. **FA:** Bob Gaines and Charlie Peterson, 1990.

9. The Consolation Direct (5.10b) ** Although this route has some loose rock, pitches 2, 3, and 4 offer great crack climbing, and the direct finish adds perhaps the best and most exciting moves of the route. Do the first two pitches of *Constellation* for a direct start and you'll have an even better route. **Pitch 1:** Begin with some 4th-class climbing up and left to a bushy corner system, then climb right-facing flakes (5.1) up to a belay ledge on the left (165 feet). **Pitch 2:** Climb cracks up to the main left-facing dihedral (many variations possible), taking care passing some very loose blocks, to a belay at a small ledge on the right. **Pitch 3:** Jam up the corner (5.9-) to a belay at a big, sloping ledge on the right. **Pitch 4:** Continue with strenuous jamming (5.9) up the left-facing dihedral to ledges, where you can traverse up and right to *The Long Climb* or left to *Whodunit*. **Pitch 5:** Climb up and right to a belay at the base of a deep vertical slot. **Pitch 6:** Jam the slot (strenuous 5.10a), then climb over a roof (5.10a/b) to a belay about 10 feet higher. **Pitch 7:** Easier climbing up the crack through several small overlaps takes you to the top. **Pro:** to 3 inches. **FA:** (5.8, A1) John Mendenhall and Chuck Wilts, May 1953. **FFA:** Royal Robbins and TM Herbert, 1959. **FA, Direct finish:** Unknown.

Northwest Recess—Upper Pitches

10. Farewell Horizontal (5.10c) ** A long, sustained face pitch with lots of great moves. Begin just left of *Wong Climb* at a white dike. A bolt protects a 5.9 section up to loose flakes; climb over an overlap up to another bolt. Follow a flake system until it peters out, where five more bolts protect 5.10 face climbing up to a ledge with a 2-bolt anchor. **Descent:** Rappel with

Northwest Recess Face Routes

two ropes (150 feet). **Pro:** thin nuts to 2-inch CDs. **FA:** Tom Beck and Scott Escher, July 1998.

11. The Sting (5.11c) * This route climbs the steep face left of the second pitch of *The Long Climb*. Begin at the 2-bolt anchor for *Farewell Horizontal* and climb a flake up to a steep, difficult face (5.11b/c) with four bolts, moving right after the fourth bolt up to a tiny ledge. Traverse left (5.10-) past a fifth bolt over to a crack that is followed up to a 2-bolt anchor. **Descent:** Rappel 100 feet to the *Farewell Horizontal* bolt anchor, then 150 feet to the ground. **Pro:** medium nuts and CDs to 2.5 inches. **FA:** Bob Gaines and Frank Bentwood, October 1999.

12. The Long Climb (5.8) ** One of the early classics, with some memorable passages, first done by none other than Royal Robbins. At the far right corner of the Northwest Recess are two long, parallel cracks that merge several hundred feet up the cliff. **Pitch 1:** The best start is to climb the left crack (called the *Wong Climb*), a great 5.8 jam crack. The right crack (5.5) is the original *Long Climb* start. Either crack ends at a nice ledge with a two-bolt anchor (150-foot rappel). **Pitch 2:** (5.7) Climb the left crack system, the infamous Mummy Crack, to a wide, sloping ledge. (The *Wong Climb* goes up the crack on the right, which is a rather unpleasant 5.8 squeeze chimney with loose chockstones.)

The Mummy Crack can be climbed as a strenuous squeeze chimney or as a steep lieback. At the top of the Mummy Crack, continue up cracks past a small overhang, to a belay at a big, sloping ledge. **Pitch 3:** Jam a crack on the right (5.7) and work up to and over another overhang, then climb to a nice belay ledge on the left just above a huge, dead mountain mahogany. **Pitch 4:** Climb a short pitch up and left across a friction slab (5.6 R), then back up and right over a flake to a belay at a pine tree (fir). You can avoid the runout slab by climbing straight up a left-facing corner, over a small roof, up another dihedral, then traversing right to the pine tree belay (5.6). **Pitch 5:** Climb about 40 feet up a trough to a downward-jutting, V-shaped block; move around its left side (5.8), then climb 10 feet up a little left-facing corner forming its left side (5.8). Traverse right to a crack that is followed (5.6) up to a belay ledge above at a V notch. **Pitch 6:** Climb diagonally up and right (5.5) to the top. **Pro:** to 3.5 inches. **FA:** Royal Robbins and Don Wilson, May 1952. **FA, Wong Climb:** Tom Higgins, et al., 1963.

13. Special K (5.10d R) ** An exciting face pitch up the narrow slab between the *Wong Climb* and *The Long Climb*'s first pitches. Climb unprotected face (5.7) up to a flake system, up this (5.9) to a friction slab (5.10+), then up a short headwall (5.10+) finish to a 2-bolt belay/rappel

anchor (150 feet). Beware of rope drag that can hinder you on the very delicate climbing on the pitch's top half. **Pro:** thin to 2 inches, six bolts, one fixed pin. **FA:** Bob Gaines and Frank Bentwood, October 1999.

Northwest Recess—Lower Right Side

Steve Schwartz rounds the "Doubtful Corner" on *White Maiden's Walkway* PHOTO BOB GAINES

5.

Maiden Buttress

This prominent 1,000-foot-high buttress separates the Northwest Recess and the West Face Bulge. The long, moderate classic *White Maiden's Walkway* starts on the left side of the Maiden Buttress and ascends the buttress to the top of the rock. *The Illegitimate* climbs the left side of the Maiden Buttress, joining *White Maiden's Walkway* about halfway up the cliff. Several one-pitch slab routes are located on the left side of the toe of the buttress, known as the White Maiden's Apron, and several steep and difficult one-pitch routes are located on the lower right side of the Maiden Buttress, facing Lunch Rock. The Maiden Buttress can be seen as the left edge of the rock when viewed from Lunch Rock.

Approach: The approach to the Maiden Buttress can be made from either the North Side Trail or the Lunch Rock Trail.

From the Lunch Rock Trail: From Lunch Rock, walk straight left on talus, then on a rough trail; the Maiden Buttress's right side is directly ahead. To get to the left side of the buttress, to the start of *Illegitimate, White Maiden's Walkway,* and the White Maiden's Apron, walk along the very base of the buttress, scramble up and over a notch, then scramble a short distance uphill.

From the North Side Trail: Where the North Side Trail first reaches the base of the cliff, walk right along the base of the Northeast Face, then a few hundred feet uphill and to the right of the North Buttress to reach the Northwest Recess. The Maiden Buttress is just right of the Northwest Recess, extending several hundred feet lower and forming a low point on the cliff face.

Descent: Descent can be made by using either the Friction Route or the North Gully—it takes roughly the same amount of time to descend either route and return to the base.

1. The Illegitimate (5.9+) ** Another Royal Robbins 1950s classic with a wild and intimidating crux pitch up the steep left side of the Maiden Buttress. **Pitch 1:** Climb the first section of *White Maiden's Walkway* (5.4) and belay at the start of the long, diagonal crack, near a tree. **Pitch 2:** Lieback and jam the left-leaning crack (5.8) for about 100 feet, until you can hand traverse right to a belay stance at a tiny ledge with less than perfect

Maiden Buttress

White Maiden's Apron

anchors. Another option is to set up a belay with big cams (3 inches) at a small ledge a bit higher in the main crack. **Pitch 3:** (190 feet) Continue up the crack system to steep and unobvious face climbing (5.9+), then jam a crack in the corner to an improbable move right over the dihedral at a downward-jutting flake (about 15 feet below some old fixed pins). Make a delicate and exposed face traverse (5.9) up and right for about 30 feet to a left-facing corner. Follow the corner up to the belay tree shared with *White Maiden's Walkway,* which is followed to the top. **Pro:** extra slings, nuts, and at least two each CDs from 0.3 to 3 inches, plus one 3.5 inches. **FA:** Royal Robbins and TM Herbert, May 1959.

2. White Maiden's Walkway (5.4) **

Popular for good reason, as it is one of Tahquitz's longest moderate routes, with lots of great climbing. The only thing that detracts from its greatness is a bit of awkward maneuvering through trees and bushes. There are a myriad of variations to this route; the route described here is the one I've found to be most straightforward and enjoyable. The climb ascends the wide buttress that is seen as the left edge of the cliff when viewed from Lunch Rock. Begin at the left side of the Maiden Buttress, at the highest pine tree at the far right corner of the Northwest Recess. This tree can be reached via 3rd-class ledges from the right, or approached directly via unprotected 4th-class slabs from below. **Pitch 1:** Climb steep corners and flakes (5.4) just right of the tree up to ledges with several pine trees, above which is a large flake resting at the base of a dihedral. An alternate start is about 40 feet to the right, up a crack (5.6) in a small right-facing trough/corner. **Pitch 2:** Climb the left-facing dihedral, exiting right at the top to comfortable ledges. The clean, straight-in crack just left of the dihedral makes for an excellent 5.7 variation to this pitch. **Pitch 3:** Climb the shallow gully on the right, which steepens into several shallow, smooth dihedrals. Where progress becomes difficult, make an improbable reach out to the right, exiting the corner (5.4), then climb about 15 feet up to a belay at a ledge with a huge mountain mahogany. **Pitch 4:** Work left past bushes, then climb about 50 feet up a clean right-facing dihedral. Traverse straight left, taking care as you pass a loose block, then make the improbable and exposed move left around the "Doubtful Corner" to a belay stance at a tree. The tree is less than bomber, although you can belay standing on the curved trunk of the tree with anchors just above it. You can also belay about 40 feet higher at a sloping ledge with a mountain mahogany. **Pitch 5:** Climb a right-facing corner for about 80 feet to a big tree, then continue diagonally up and right to a belay at another large tree. **Pitch 6:** Climb a short, 4th-class pitch up and right on a flake to a belay ledge just below the summit overhangs. **Pitch 7:** One of the most exciting pitches on the route! Climb a few feet up a crack, then move right under the big arch that curves right, crossing over another smaller overhang (below the main arch) on its right side (5.3), finishing with slab climbing to the top. For a more difficult finish, climb straight up from the initial crack, following the crack through roofs (5.7). **Pro:** to 3 inches. **FA:** Jim Smith and Arthur Johnson, August 1937.

3. Zeno's Paradox (5.11a) ** This excellent variation begins from the ledges at the top the second pitch of *Illegitimate*. Belay on the right side of the ledge at the base of a thin crack. Jam a vegetated fingertip crack (5.10a) up to a strenuous lieback up a left-facing corner that arches left. (It's the left of two very similar left-facing corners, covered in green lichen.) Above the arch, climb up and right on a steep face (5.11a) past two bolts up to the left-facing corner of *Illegitimate*. **Pro:** thin to 3.5 inches, including several CDs from 2 to 3.5 inches. **FA:** Kevin Powell, Spencer Lennard, and Chris Robbins, 1978.

WHITE MAIDEN'S APRON

This is the slabby skirt forming the lowest point on the left base of the Maiden Buttress. It gets shade in the afternoon. On a crowded weekend it also provides a viewing area where you can be entertained by the climbing antics on the Northwest Recess, out of the rockfall zone.

Approach: Follow the North Side Trail up to the Maiden Buttress—the White Maiden's Apron is the slab that extends out to the toe of the buttress on the right. From Lunch Rock, walk straight left on talus, then on a rough trail—the Maiden Buttress is directly ahead. Walk along the base of the buttress, scramble up and over a notch, then scramble a short distance uphill.

Descent: From the top of the slab, a short downclimb leads to a rappel tree (80 feet).

1. Iron Maiden (5.12a) * Begin on the apron's far left side and climb a thin slab (5.12a above the second bolt), then climb through roofs and finish up a slab, passing six more bolts along the way. **Pro:** 0.4-inch TCUs, gear anchor from 1.5 to 2 inches. **FA:** Bob Gaines and Charlie Peterson, July 1990.

2. Maiden Heaven (5.10c) * Begin about 30 feet right of *Iron Maiden*. Climb the face just left of a right-facing corner (5.10b) past a bolt (or climb the corner, 5.7 R), then up the slab past six more bolts to the top. **Pro:** gear anchor from 1.5 to 2 inches. **FA:** Bob Gaines and Charlie Peterson, July 1990.

3. Maiden Voyage (5.10d) * Start 30 feet right of *Maiden Heaven* at a flake. Climb the slab (5.10d), traversing right

White Maiden's Apron

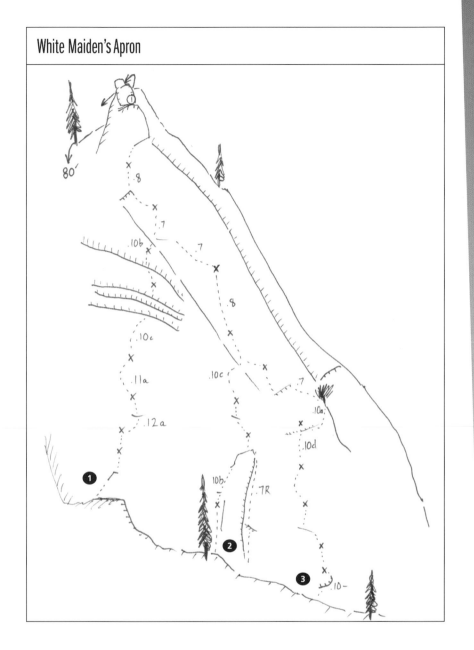

at the fifth bolt, then up to the corner on the right (2-inch CD). Traverse left (5.7) and up past five more bolts (5.8) to the top. **Pro:** 2-inch CD, gear anchor from 1.5 to 2 inches. **FA:** Bob Gaines, Kelly Vaught, and Frank Bentwood, October 2009.

MAIDEN BUTTRESS— LOWER RIGHT SIDE

The following three routes are located on the short, steep wall forming the lower right side of the Maiden Buttress, easily visible from Lunch Rock. To approach these routes, scramble (4th class) up a gully directly below the cliff.

Descent: Rappel 80 feet.

1. Zuma (5.12a) * Traverse left on a flake to start and climb up over a bulge (5.10d) to a bolt that protects a bizarre sequence of moves (5.12a). Follow the crack to a flake that curves right, then move left to a bolt (5.11a) that protects face climbing up to a 2-bolt anchor. **Pro:** thin nuts, TCUs and CDs from 0.4 to 2.5 inches. **FA:** Bob Gaines and Charlie Peterson, August 1990.

2. Stinger (5.11d) * Start about 50 feet up the gully from *Zuma*. Power through an overhanging bulge (5.11d) past two bolts to a thin crack with two fixed pins, then up to a 2-bolt belay/rappel anchor. **Pro:** medium nuts, CDs from 0.4-inch to 2 inches. **FA:** Bob Gaines and Dave Mayville, August 1993.

3. One Nut Willie (5.11d) * Begin about 50 feet uphill from *Stinger* at the base of a deep chimney that leads to the crest of the lower Maiden Buttress. Power up an overhanging lieback (5.11d), then stem past two bolts (5.11b). Move right (5.10b) around the corner to a third bolt, then face climb and mantle (5.10b) up to a 2-bolt belay/rappel anchor. **Pro:** to 2 inches. **FA:** Bob Gaines and Dave Mayville, July 1993.

Maiden Buttress—Lower Right Side

6

West Face Bulge

This monolithic headwall is the steepest and most exposed sector of Tahquitz Rock, featuring some of the very best routes, including *The Vampire* (5.11a), considered by many climbers to be *the* best climb in Southern California. During the summer this wall remains shady all morning long and gets sun in the afternoon.

Approach: The Lunch Rock Trail is commonly used to access the West Face Bulge. The routes can be approached in two ways. The *From Bad Traverse* is an approach route that begins from *The Trough* and climbs diagonally up and left to the start of the routes. Another, more direct approach for *The Step, Le Toit, Le Toitlette,* and *Super Pooper* is to climb the easy 5th-class gully just right of the Maiden Buttress's lower right side, then climb *Standup Flake* (5.9) up to ledges below *Le Toit.*

***From Bad Traverse* approach:** The route that crosses from the top

West Face Bulge Overview

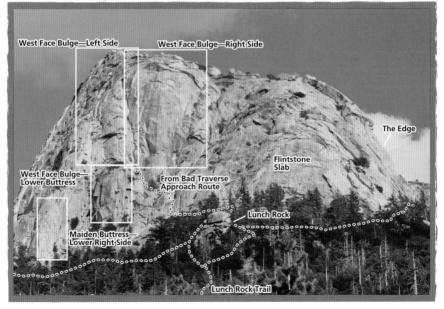

of *The Trough*'s first pitch, leading up and left across ledges and ramps to the big ledge beneath the roof of *Le Toit* is known as *From Bad Traverse* (5.6). From Lunch Rock, walk up talus and a rough trail directly to the base of the rock (just right of *Angel's Fright*). Just left of *Angel's Fright*, scramble up a few feet, then squeeze through a short chimney, or make an exposed move left around the corner (4th class), then up a little slab back to the base. Walk left along the base (beneath Scarface Slab) and past *Dave's Deviation* to the start of *The Trough* gully. Climb the first pitch of *The Trough* (5.3), then climb up and left to a ledge with trees. Continue up and left (5.6) on a blocky ramp to a ledge with mountain mahogany bushes. To approach the West Face Bulge—Right Side routes (*The Flakes, Stairway to Heaven, The Vampire,* and *The Crucifix*), climb a short right-facing corner (5.7) directly above this point to reach a large, flat ledge (called Vampire Ledge). To get to the base of the West Face Bulge—Left Side routes (*The Step, Le Toit, Le Toitlette,* and *Super Pooper*), continue up and left (5.6) from the mountain mahogany bushes to reach a series of ledges with bushes and a prominent, large, sprawling pine tree. These ledges are directly below the obvious roof of *Le Toit*.

Descent: The Friction Route.

WEST FACE BULGE—LEFT SIDE

1. The Step (5.10a/b PG) ** This route breaks through the line of overhangs about 40 feet left of *Le Toit*. Start from the big ledge below the roofs. **Pitch 1:** Climb a right-facing corner up to and through the intimidating roof (5.10-), then lieback a unique crack inside a crack that leads to a left-facing dihedral. Step left to a thin flake/corner, then move back right to an awkward mantle (5.9+) and belay about 15 feet higher at tiny ledges (1.5- to 3-inch CDs). **Pitch 2:** Undercling, lieback, and jam (5.8-) the spectacular flake that arches right. Where the flake ends, face climb up to a belay ledge with a mountain mahogany. **Pitch 3:** From here you can work right up a ramp to a left-facing corner and finish up *Super Pooper* or traverse left to an easier finish up *White Maiden's Walkway*. **Pro:** thin to 4 inches, including three each CDs from 1.5 to 2 inches, two 3 inches and one 4 inches. **FA:** Royal Robbins and Jerry Gallwas, 1957. **FFA:** Royal Robbins and TM Herbert, 1959.

2. Le Toit (5.12a R) *** One of the classic aid routes from the 1960s, this route free climbs one of Tahquitz's largest roofs. The R is given as a warning for the unprotected 5.8 mantle at the start, from which a fall would be disastrous. **Pitch 1:** Climb loose flakes to an unprotected 5.8 mantle, then face climb past a bolt (5.10+) to flakes that lead up to a 3-bolt hanging belay at the start of a left-curving arch.

Tony Sartin on the crux roof of *Le Toit* (5.12a)
Photo Greg Epperson

Pitch 2: Up the arch (5.10d), then jam over the roof at fixed pins (5.12-) and face climb (5.10c) up to a 2-bolt hanging belay. Pitches 1 and 2 can be easily done in one pitch. Rappel from here (100 feet) or continue. **Pitch 3:** Follow the arch all the way to the right (5.10c), then climb straight up, joining *Super Pooper*. **Pro:** thin to medium nuts, TCUs, plus one each CD from 1.5 to 3 inches. **FA:** (A3) TM Herbert, Tom Frost, and Yvon Chouinard, March 1960. **FFA:** John Long and Rick Accomazzo, 1973.

3. Pooper Scooper (aka Denny's Variation) (5.11c) ** This is a direct finish to *Le Toit*, originally named after Denny Adams, who took a very long fall on the first attempt of this route. It was renamed by Erik Roed after the FFA, when a climber mistakenly asked him, "Did you climb *Pooper Scooper*?" when he meant *Super Pooper*. At *Le Toit*'s third pitch, climb directly up to the arch and over a small overhang (5.11c) at a thin crack with fixed pins. Move left to a flake, clip a bolt, then traverse right to another flake. Angle up and right on the slab to *Super Pooper*. **Pro:** to 2 inches. **FA:** (5.9, A2) Dave Black and Alan Bartlett, June 1972. **FFA:** Erik Roed and Jason Lanman.

4. Le Toitlette (5.11c) ** Start just right of *Le Toit*. Climb up to a bolt, then step right and up (5.10d) a tiny corner. Follow thin flakes up and left to a second bolt that protects very thin moves on a smooth face (5.11d) leading up and left to a crack. Follow this up to a little roof, then move left under the roof (the crack on the right side is unprotectable 5.9) and climb through the ceilings (5.9) up to an easier crack that takes you to a belay on *Super Pooper*. **Pro:** thin to 2 inches. **FA:** Charles Cole and Craig Fry, August 1985.

5. Super Pooper (5.10b) *** A beautiful line up soaring dihedrals. **Pitch 1:** Several different crack systems (none harder than 5.9) lead to a belay at a good ledge at the base of a left-facing corner. **Pitch 2:** Climb the crack, past a wedged chockstone and a fixed pin,

up to a small roof. Turn the roof on the left, then make delicate moves up to a tiny ledge (5.10-). A difficult fist jam leads up to another chockstone, followed by strenuous hand jamming in the back of a flare (5.10-). Traverse left, when possible, to another crack and follow it a short distance to a belay stance at the base of a thin crack on the left wall of the dihedral. **Pitch 3:** Jam thin finger cracks on the left wall (5.8) onto an arête, then belay at a small stance at the base of a dihedral/ramp capped with a small roof. At this point you can traverse right (5.8) across the face for the *Price of Fear* (5.10c) finish. **Pitch 4:** Watch out for rope drag on this long pitch. Lieback the corner (5.7), turn the roof on the left (5.8-), then stay left as you approach a bulge. Work back right, then climb up and left through the bulge at a weakness onto unprotected (5.6) slab climbing to the top. **Pro:** thin to 3 inches, including two each CDs from 0.4 to 3 inches, plus three 2 inches. **FA:** Chuck Wilts, Don Wilson, John and Ruth Mendenhall, September 1952. **FFA:** Bob Kamps and Mark Powell, 1967.

6. The Price of Fear (5.10c) ** A spectacular and airy pitch that is a great direct finish for *Super Pooper* or *The Flakes*. It can be accessed by traversing right from the start of *Super Pooper's* third pitch, or traversing left from *The Flakes's* third pitch. Follow an arête with a thin crack up to three

bolts that protect delicate face climbing to the top. **FA:** Milo Prodanovich and Steve McKinny, 1969. **FFA:** Tobin Sorenson and Matt Cox, 1972.

WEST FACE BULGE—RIGHT SIDE

1. The Flakes (5.11c) ** (*** with *Price of Fear* finish) Start from the ledge at the top of *Super Pooper's* first pitch. **Pitch 1:** (5.11a) Climb a very thin, tricky to protect (tiny nuts and TCUs) flake up to just below a small roof, then stem right and power over the roof up to a small belay ledge with a mountain mahogany. **Pitch 2:** (5.8) Climb a short distance up the right-facing dihedral (*Stairway to Heaven* climbs straight up this dihedral, 5.10a), then step left and climb a spectacular flake system that diagonals up and left from the main corner. Belay at a nice ledge with two bolts (shared with *Stairway to Heaven*). **Pitch 3:** Up a short right-facing corner to the top of a pillar, then clip a high bolt. Make a long, height-dependent reach, or crank a bouldery dynamic move off thin sidepulls. Climb up and left to a belay at the base of a huge right-curving arch. **Pitch 4:** For a classic and exciting finish, move left and climb *The Price of Fear* to the top. The original route diagonals 80 feet right across an exposed 5.7 friction slab, then climbs through a weakness near the apex of the arch (5.9, same finish as *The Vampire*) to the

West Face Bulge—Right Side Overview

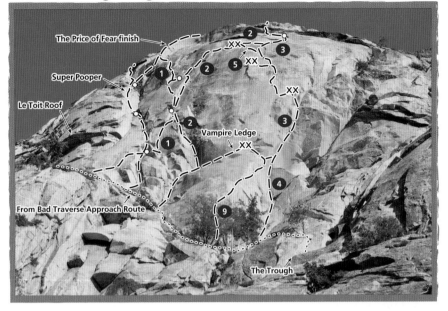

The Price of Fear finish

Super Pooper

Le Toit Roof

Vampire Ledge

From Bad Traverse Approach Route

The Trough

top. **FA:** Royal Robbins and Don Wilson, July 1953. **FFA:** John Long, Tobin Sorenson, Richard Harrison, and Bill Antel, 1973.

2. Stairway to Heaven (5.12a) *** The demanding first pitch is one of the great leads of Tahquitz Rock, although the more well-protected third pitch is technically the crux. Start from the left side of Vampire Ledge. **Pitch 1:** Lieback a 4- to 5-inch-wide crack (5.9) up the dihedral, then stem and face climb (5.11b) up to a bolt. You can get a good rest before the crux if you downclimb a bit to a stance on the left. Crank a slightly overhanging face on incuts (5.11d), moving up and left to a belay ledge at the base

of a right-facing dihedral shared with *The Flakes.* **Pitch 2:** Lieback and jam the dihedral (5.10a) up to a good ledge with a 2-bolt anchor. **Pitch 3:** Power up and right past two bolts to an arch (5.12a), then up a thin crack to a bolt. Face climb straight right (5.11b) over to a flake (small to medium stopper), then make a final step right (5.11a) over to a 2-bolt belay. **Pitch 4:** Move down and right across a slab (5.10b; R for follower) to join *The Vampire.* The original route uses aid from a bolt above the belay to reach 5.9 face climbing. **Pro:** to 4.5 inches, including several from 3 to 4.5 inches. **FA:** (5.9, A4) Dave Black, Dave Hamburg, and Mike Graber, September 1973. **FFA:** John Long and Bob Gaines, July 1984.

3. The Vampire (5.11a) *** A magnificent climb that achieves a dramatic, exposed position on the West Face Bulge. Perhaps the best route on Tahquitz. **Pitch 1:** From the 2-bolt anchor on the right side of Vampire Ledge, traverse down and right to reach the strenuous Bat Crack. Hand jamming (5.9) leads to fingertip jamming and liebacking (5.10c). Easier climbing leads to a bolt that protects a hard move (5.11a) in the crack. Above this you can place pro high in the crack to protect a committing face move/mantle up to a 3-bolt belay stance. **Pitch 2:** Make a thin and delicate face move down and left (5.11a) to reach a thin flake. Lieback the spectacular flake (5.10a) and jam past a big loose flake, then traverse left across "the batwalk" to a hanging belay at bolts. **Pitch 3:** Traverse right, back to the flake, then climb up until you can reach right to clip a bolt. Step right and climb a very thin crack that slants up and right (5.11a, height dependent to start), then climb flakes up and right to an arching corner. You can set up a belay at a tiny ledge where you first get to the corner (2- to 3-inch CDs), or a bit higher at a hanging belay under the arch where it first curves left (1.5- to 2-inch CDs). The crux section at the thin crack can be avoided by moving 15 feet down and right from the bolt, then back up and left on slab moves to join the thin crack (5.10c). **Pitch 4:** Climb flakes and cracks up to and through a line of weakness in the overhangs (5.9) to the top. **Pro:** small nuts and CDs to 3 inches, including many 1.5- and 2-inch CDs. **FA:** (5.9, A3) Royal Robbins and Dave Rearick, June 1959. **FFA:** John Long, Rick Accomazzo, Mike Graham, and Bill Antel, 1973.

4. Vampire Direct Start (5.10d) * Start at a ledge with a big pine tree on the *From Bad Traverse* approach and climb the steep crack in a brown dihedral directly up to the Bat Crack. **FA:** Unknown.

5. Vampire Direct Finish (5.10c R) * The lieback flake on this exhilarating variation becomes so thin that a fall on pro might break it! At the bolt on the third pitch of *The Vampire,* where *The Vampire* moves right up the thin crack, the direct finish continues up the flake. Undercling and lieback (gingerly) the precarious flake (5.10c), which becomes wafer thin, up to a 2-bolt belay shared with *Stairway to Heaven.* From this belay, climb down and right (5.10b; R for follower) to reconnect with *The Vampire.* **FA:** Tim Sorenson, 1970s.

6. The Crucifix (5.11c) *** From the end of *The Vampire*'s Bat Crack, climb down and right (5.10c) to a small, flat ledge with a 2-bolt anchor. *The Bat* traverses around the corner to the left. *The Crucifix* climbs the steep dihedral directly above the belay ledge past two bolts (5.11c), up over a little roof,

then up a thin crack/face past two more bolts to a fifth bolt. Move left here, with tough face moves (5.11c) across a band of gold rock up to a 2-bolt hanging belay. **Pro:** thin nuts, TCUs and CDs from 0.4 to .75 inch. **FA:** (A2) Unknown. **FFA:** Bob Gaines and Tommy Romero, August 1995.

7. Field of Dreams (5.11d) *** High-quality slab climbing in a stunning location. Combine *The Vampire*'s Bat Crack with *The Crucifix* to *Field of Dreams* for a Tahquitz classic. From the hanging belay on *The Bat,* climb up and left to *The Bat*'s first bolt, then climb straight up the beautiful slab past six more bolts to a belay at the arch (1- to 3-inch CDs). Follow *Upper Royal's Arch* to the top. **FA:** Bob Gaines and Charlie Peterson, August 1996.

8. The Bat (5.11c R) ** **Pitch 1:** At the top of *The Vampire*'s Bat Crack, climb down and right (5.10c) to a nice, flat belay ledge with two bolts. **Pitch 2:** Traverse around the corner to the left, lieback a steep crack to an old bolt ladder, clip the first bolt, then traverse right and up past two bolts, moving left and up (5.11c) across a band of gold rock to a two-bolt hanging belay. **Pitch 3:** Friction up and left on a white ramp past two bolts (5.11a), join *The Vampire* briefly at its left-facing corner, then face climb up and right to a belay at a tiny ledge. **Pitch 4:** Climb up the slab (5.10a) to join *Upper Royal's Arch* as it climbs over the head-wall. **Pro:** several to 3 inches. **FA, with bolt ladder:** (5.7, A2) Don Wilson, Jerry Gallwas, and Chuck Wilts, 1960 (they pendulumed right from the top of the bolt ladder). **FFA, dihedral to bolt ladder:** Tobin Sorenson, 1973. **FA, complete route:** Bob Gaines and Yvonne Gaines, September 1987.

9. The Pharaoh (5.12b) * No topo. Start from the *From Bad Traverse,* at a ledge with a big pine tree. Jam the arching, sustained thin crack on the right side of the steep face below Vampire Ledge. **Pro:** many thin to 3.5 inches. **FA:** Lynn Hill and John Long, 1983.

WEST FACE BULGE— LOWER BUTTRESS

This is the section of cliffs directly below the start of *Le Toit* and *The Step*. From Lunch Rock, walk left for about 200 feet, then climb cracks and slabs (easy 5th class) up the right side of the wide gully just right of the Maiden Buttress's lower right side for several hundred feet up to a ledge at the base of the routes.

1. Le Toit Direct (5.8) * Climb the crack in the left-facing dihedral just left of *Slapstick*. **Pro:** to 3 inches. **FA:** Unknown.

2. Slapstick (5.12c) ** Perhaps Tahquitz's most demanding arête pitch. Sustained and very well protected. Lieback and slap your way up the rounded arête past nine bolts. The sequential crux is passing the fourth and fifth bolts. The remainder of the pitch offers sustained 5.11 climbing up much of the arête. A 1-inch CD is useful before the first bolt. **Descent:** Make a 100-foot rappel. **FA:** Dave Mayville and Bob Gaines, May 1999.

3. Standup Flake (5.9) * This pitch makes a great direct start to *Le Toit*. Lieback and jam the vertical flake/crack just to the right of *Slapstick*. **Pro:** to 3 inches. **FA:** Unknown.

West Face Bulge—Lower Buttress

West Face Overview

Lunch Ledge

Flintstone Slab

Angel's Fright

Center

Scarface Slab

Pine Tree Ledge

Dave's Deviation

Left Side

The Trough

7.

West Face

This is the section of Tahquitz Rock directly above Lunch Rock, bordered on the left side by the large corner that runs diagonally up and right (*The Trough,* 5.4) and on the right by the gigantic arête of *The Edge*. Many of the routes on the center of the face converge at Lunch Ledge, several hundred feet up the face directly above Lunch Rock and 10 feet above a prominent, solitary pine tree. The West Face stays in the shade for most of the morning, making it a good place for an early start on a hot day.

Approach: In this book the West Face is divided into several sections: Left Side, Scarface Slab, Center, Flintstone Slab, and Right Side. Approach information is included with each section.

Descent: The Friction Route is the standard descent. Numerous rappel routes from either trees or bolt anchors are possible on the West Face, and are identified in the route descriptions and topos.

WEST FACE—LEFT SIDE

This section includes the routes from *The Trough* to Scarface Slab.

Approach: From Lunch Rock, walk straight up to the base of the cliff to the start of *Angel's Fright* (the first pitch can be identified as a vertical chimney crack). Scramble up and left (tunnel under a chockstone and up a short chimney, or make a more exposed 4th-class move on a slab a bit to the left), then walk left across a ledge at the base of Scarface Slab, past the start of *Dave's Deviation* to a prominent break in the cliff. *The Trough* and *Dave's Deviation* converge at Pine Tree Ledge, an area with several wide ledges, easily identified by a 50-foot-high pine tree growing at the ledge (the largest pine tree on this section of the cliff).

West Face—Left Side

1. The Trough (5.4) ** This moderate classic was the first route climbed on Tahquitz, and for many climbers, their first introduction to multi-pitch trad climbing. **Pitch 1:** (5.3) Rope up at the far left end of the ledge below *Dave's Deviation* and jam a low-angle crack that leads around the corner to the left. The crack widens before ending at a big, sloping ledge. **Pitch 2:** (5.3) Friction up and left across a short slab, then stem and jam your way up cracks in the namesake "trough" to a small ledge on the right (1.5- to 2-inch CDs useful for the anchor). **Pitch 3:** Continue up the crack system, through an awkward bulge in the crack (5.4); where the corner steepens, traverse right and climb up to Pine Tree Ledge. **Pitch 4:** Face climb a steep wall with huge holds up to an oak tree (optional belay), then head up a 4th-class chute to the top (180 feet). **Pro:** to 3 inches. **FA:** Jim Smith, Bob Brinton, and Z. Jasaitis, August 1936.

2. Piton Pooper to Upper Royal's Arch

(5.8) ** Combine these two routes with the *Dave's Deviation* start for a Tahquitz classic. The upper arch has exhilarating exposure. **Pitch 1:** (*Piton Pooper*) From the lower left end of Pine Tree Ledge, reach left and climb a steep, classic dihedral (5.7+), then move up and left to a

belay at a tree. **Pitch 2:** Climb a short pitch up and left to a belay stance just left of a prominent pine tree, at the base of the arch that caps the top of the West Face Bulge. **Pitch 3:** (*Upper Royal's Arch*) Climb up the arch for about 40 feet, to where the crack thins. Make an unobvious traverse down and left about 15 feet onto a very exposed face, then climb up and right on the slab (5.8), working back over to the main arch. Climbing directly up the dihedral is also possible (5.10b PG). Follow the crack in the arch for about 50 more feet, until you can cross over it at a flake (5.8), then climb up to and over a short, overhanging dihedral (5.8, TCUs) to the top. **Pro:** thin to 3 inches. **FA, *Piton Pooper* (A2):** Bob Brinton and Andy Johnson, September 1936. **FFA:** Chuck Wilts, Ellen Wilts, and Spencer Austin, 1949. **FA, *Upper Royal's Arch:*** Royal Robbins, Jerry Gallwas, and Chuck Wilts, 1953.

Piton Pooper to Upper Royal's Arch

3. The Rack (5.10a) * **Pitch 1:** Climb up *The Trough* for about 30 feet, then move right and climb the slab past two bolts (5.10a) to corners that lead to a right-facing dihedral. Belay at a ledge near the end of the corner. **Pitch 2:** Climb a slab and cracks that lead up and right to Pine Tree Ledge. **Pro:** thin to 3 inches. **FA:** Bob Kamps, Mark Powell, and Beverly Powell, 1961.

4. Legends of the Fall (5.10c PG) ** **Pitch 1:** Begin by climbing a few feet up *The Trough,* then traverse right to a thin crack system (just left of *The Jam Crack*'s left-facing dihedral). Follow the crack until it peters out, then face climb up to and over the left side of a little roof and follow a thin flake until it ends. Committing face climbing (5.9) up and left leads to a bolt. Traverse straight left (5.10a), then follow a right-facing flake that curves right. Clip another bolt that protects runout face climbing up a thin flake (5.9 PG) to a third bolt. Above this, a bolt protects tricky moves over an overhang (5.10c). Belay a few feet higher at a 2-bolt stance (115 feet). **Pitch 2:** Friction past two bolts, moving right (5.9) at the second bolt, then climb up (5.7 PG) to a flake (3-inch CD) and a bolt that protects a step-up (5.9) over a small roof. Continue up an unprotected but easy slab to a few 5.6 moves through overlapping flakes up to Pine Tree Ledge (115 feet). You can rappel the route from here in two 115-foot rappels with a 70-meter

rope, but you'll probably need slings for the pine tree (3-foot diameter). **Pro:** thin nuts, CDs from 0.3 to 3 inches, including many 0.3 to .75 inch. **FA:** Bob Gaines, Kelly Vaught, and Frank Bentwood, September 2009.

5. The Jam Crack (5.8 PG) ** **Pitch 1:** Begin just to the right of *The Trough* in a deep crack that turns into a left-facing corner with a small roof. Jam the crack, turn the roof on the left, then continue up the crack until you can traverse right to the 3-bolt anchor shared with *Dave's Deviation* (100-foot rappel). **Pitch 2:** Continue on *Dave's Deviation* to the top. **Pro:** thin to 2.5 inches. **FA:** Royal Robbins and Don Wilson, September 1959.

6. Manwich (5.11a PG) * After the first 20 feet of *Dave's Deviation,* climb straight up the slab past two bolts, moving right at the top to join *Dave's Deviation* just below the ledge. **Pro:** to 2 inches. **FA:** Terry Ayers, Craig Fry, and Jack Marshall, June 1986.

7. Sweedish Variation (5.10d TR) * From the first bolt of *Manwich,* reach left and slap and smear your way up the arête. **FA:** Bob Gaines and Chip Jewlet, August 2004.

8. Dave's Deviation (5.9) *** The first pitch is one of the best 5.9 finger cracks in Idyllwild. **Pitch 1:** Begin just right of the deep crack of *The Jam*

Pine Tree Ledge

Crack. Lieback a steep flake on the right, then climb the classic thin finger crack with a mountain mahogany growing out of it, up to a small ledge with a 3-bolt anchor (100-foot rappel). **Pitch 2:** Lieback the flake on the right, then face climb up and left to a crack that leads to a bulging arch. Face climb a few feet up and right, then back left (5.8 PG) to gain a flake. Move right again, then climb past several overlapping arches up to Pine Tree Ledge (165 feet). **Pro:** thin to 2 inches. **FA:** Tom Frost and Royal Robbins, 1960.

9. Dave's Deviation Direct Start

(5.10c) * This more difficult start begins 20 feet right of the regular route. Climb around the left side of a small overhang up to a bolt (5.10c), then move up and left (5.10b) to join the regular route at the start of the straight-in finger crack. **Pro:** to 2 inches. **FA:** Charlie Peterson and Bob Gaines, August 1994.

SCARFACE SLAB

This 100-foot-high, triangular slab is located about 75 feet up and left from the start of *Angel's Fright*. The routes all share a 2-bolt belay/rappel anchor at the top of the slab that is convenient for rappelling or toproping (100 feet).

1. Poker Face (5.12b or 5.8) * You can avoid the 5.12 crux by moving left below the first bolt for a 5.8 pitch. Begin 30 feet left of *Scarface*, at a crack that curves left about 30 feet up. Climb the crack (5.8) up to a bolt, then bluff your way past a blank section (5.12b) up to a second bolt that protects easier (5.6) climbing up the arête/face just right of a crack. For the 5.8 variation, where the initial crack veers left, hand traverse/jam the crack over to the corner on the left, then follow the crack (and the arête/face just to the right) up to the top. **Pro:** 0.4 to 3 inches, including several 1.5 to 2 inches. **FA:** Bob Gaines and Dave Mayville, July 1993.

Scarface Slab

The Trough

Dave's Deviation

1 2 3 4

Angel's Fright

From Lunch Rock

2. Scarface (5.11d) *** A very high-quality, four-bolt face climb up the center of the slab. The top crux is height dependent and thwarts many attempts. At the second bolt, move right (5.11c) and up to the third bolt, where the climbing eases (5.9) up to the fourth bolt. Here you can go up and left (height-dependent 5.11d) or traverse right (5.10d) over to the bolt on *Devil's Delight* for an easier finish. **FA:** Charles Cole and Bob Gaines, August 1985.

3. Devil's Delight (5.10b) ** Only the popular first pitch is described here, as the second pitch is somewhat of an unprotected horror show with

bad bolts. Start about 50 feet left of *Angel's Fright* behind a large pine tree. Lieback a steep right-facing corner, up over a slight overhang (5.10a); where the crack peters out, move left on face holds over to a tiny left-facing corner, then climb past a bolt (5.9) up to the ledge. **Pro:** to 3 inches. **FA:** Mark and Beverly Powell, August 1966.

4. Cutter (5.11b) * Begin just right of *Devil's Delight*. Climb an easy corner until you can move right to a bolt. Up an elegant crux, face climbing on incut edges up to the communal 2-bolt anchor (100 feet). The direct start is 5.10 R. **FA:** Bob Gaines and Dave Mayville, August 1993.

To Pine Tree Ledge

opt.

Lieback var.

opt.

Lunch Ledge

WEST FACE—CENTER

From Lunch Rock, walk directly uphill to the base of the rock. *Angel's Fright* can be identified by a narrow chimney leading about 40 feet up to a bushy ledge.

1. The Blank (5.10b) ** **Pitch 1:** (5.9-) Climb the short left-facing corner 20 feet left of *Angel's Fright* up to the ledge. **Pitch 2:** Climb the face (just right of the corner stacked with scary loose blocks) up to an arching roof. Climb directly over the center of the roof at a thin finger crack (5.10b), or surmount the roof at a 4-inch-wide crack/flake on its left side (5.10b), or avoid the roof completely by skirting it to the far left (5.8). Above the roof, face climb up to a flake and belay higher at a ledge with a mountain mahogany, below a prominent right-slanting dihedral. **Pitch 3:** Lieback and jam the dihedral (5.10a, 4-inch CDs), then move right to a ledge with a mountain mahogany shared with *Jonah*. **Pitch 4:** From the left side of the ledge, climb up a flake to a bolt (5.9), then traverse left to easier climbing up to a ledge, where you can traverse left to Pine Tree ledge, or right to *Jonah*. **Pro:** to 4 inches, including several 3- to 4-inch CDs. **FA:** Royal Robbins and Jerry Gallwas, May 1954. **FFA:** Tom Frost and Bob Kamps, 1960.

2. Jonah (5.10d PG/R) ** An interesting route with a variety of challenges. One of America's most difficult rock climbs when first climbed in 1964. **Pitch 1:** Begin at the short slab between *The Blank* and *Angel's Fright*. Climb a thin crack that peters out (5.10d R). **Pitch 2:** Steep and tricky. Climb to a small right-facing dihedral that turns into an overhang, then step

The Blank/Jonah, Pitch 2 Detail

right (5.10c) and up to a tiny ledge. Climb to another right-facing corner, most easily climbed by moving left off the corner, then straight up the face (5.10c) to a ledge with bushes about 30 feet higher. **Pitch 3:** (5.10a PG/R) Climb directly up to a bolt, then move right, back left, and up to a belay at a sloping ledge with bushes. **Pitch 4:** Climb a short right-facing flake to a face with two bolts. At the second bolt, make a delicate traverse 20 feet straight right (5.10b PG/R), then up to a gaping flake known as the "Whale's Mouth." The farther you go before placing pro, the more your follower will appreciate it. Chimney up and left under the flake (5.8) to a ledge (1- to 3-inch gear anchor). **Pitch 5:** Climb a short 5.9 pitch up flakes to

a left-facing corner (3- to 4-inch CDs useful) up to a higher belay ledge. **Pitch 6:** Mantle, crimp, and smear up thin edges on a slab past three bolts (5.10d) to the top. **Pro:** thin to a 4-inch CD. **FA:** Tom Higgins, Roy Coats, and M. Cohen, August 1964.

3. Angel's Fright (5.6) ** Very popular, with varied pitches, up the right-leaning, left-facing dihedral visible directly above Lunch Rock. **Pitch 1:** (5.6) Climb the strenuous chimney up to an expansive, bushy ledge. **Pitch 2:** Climb diagonally up and right on the face to the right of the ledge (5.5) to a fixed pin. When you reach the base of a small left-facing corner, move left, then climb a steep, juggy crack (5.6) up to another fixed pin. Move right

West Face—Center, Lower Pitches

and follow a crack/ramp that diagonals up and right to a small belay ledge on the right with a mountain mahogany. A nice variation is to climb the steep, juggy crack directly above the right side of the first belay ledge (5.7). **Pitch 3:** (5.0) Stem up the main corner, which resembles a chute, and belay at a ledge on the right with a big pine tree. **Pitch 4:** Climb up the dihedral, pass the overhang on the right (5.5), and climb a crack up to Lunch Ledge, just above a prominent, solitary pine tree (pitches 3 and 4 can be combined with a 60-meter rope). **Pitch 5:** From the right end of Lunch Ledge, climb past several bushy ledges (optional belay), then work up and left to a flake. Tiptoe left across the flake for about 40 feet to a mountain mahogany, then friction up a slab (5.5) past a bolt to the top (160 feet). A good variation (best done in two pitches) climbs up and right from Lunch Ledge to a belay at a big tree, then up and left on flakes to a thin, classic, low-angle fingertip lieback flake (5.6) and short friction slab to the top. **Pro:** to 3 inches. **FA:** Jim Smith and William Rice, September 1936.

4. Stage Fright (5.11b) * Climb the first crack just left of *Fright Night* up to a bolt, tiptoe left to a flake, then step right and climb a face (5.11b) past two bolts up to a ledge with a 2-bolt belay/rappel anchor (80 feet). **Pro:** thin to 4 inches. **FA:** Erik Roed, Ramone Thomson, Jason and Jon Lanman, July 2007.

5. Fright Night (5.11c) ** Climb the first right-facing dihedral just to the left of the *Human Fright* dihedral past a bolt (5.11a) up to an overhang where a second bolt protects the crux—wild liebacking and pinching

Human Fright Area

on the arête of the arching dihedral above the roof. Belay at a 2-bolt belay/rappel anchor (80 feet). **Pro:** to 2 inches. **FA:** Charles Cole and Troy Mayr, August 1988.

6. Human Fright (5.10a) ** Great crack climbing, albeit with some loose flakes. Most climbers do just the first pitch and rap off, although the second pitch is good too. **Pitch 1:** (5.10a) Climb up a clean crack in a smooth right-facing corner, then under a right-leaning, overhanging flake until you can jam up through a break in the overhang to a 2-bolt belay/rappel anchor (80 feet). **Pitch 2:** (5.10a) Climb to the huge, arching right-facing corner and jam up the corner to a belay ledge where it ends. From here you can rap from a tree (100 feet down to the 2-bolt anchor), descending in two rappels, or move left to finish on *Angel's Fright*. **Pro:** thin to 3 inches, including two each CDs from 1 to 3 inches. **FA:** John Mendenhall and Royal Robbins, June 1952. **FFA:** Bob Kamps, 1963.

LUNCH ROCK

This 60-foot-high rock, located about 200 feet directly below Tahquitz's West Face, serves as a landmark and central hub for climbers staging to climb on the West Face. The Lunch Rock Trail leads directly to this rock. From near the top of Lunch Rock, you can access a bolt anchor by tunneling through a chimney.

1. High in Protien (5.10c) This is a free version of an old aid route on the short steep wall immediately left of the *No Free Lunches* arête. Originally led with thin nuts and fixed pins, the pins are long gone, but it can be easily toproped from the *No Free Lunches* bolt anchor. **FA:** Unknown. **FFA:** Erik Roed, Ramone Thomson, Jason and Jon Lanman, July 2007.

2. No Free Lunches (5.10d) * Climb the arête just left of the *Chimney Route* past several horizontal cracks to a bolt, then move to the left side of the arête (straight up from the first bolt is 5.11+) past two more bolts up to a 2-bolt anchor (60 feet). **Pro:** to 2 inches. **FA:** Erik Roed, Ramone Thomson, Jason and Jon Lanman, July 2007.

3. Chimney Route (5.7) Climb the crack system on the main (west) face, seen directly above the approach trail. **FA:** Unknown.

4. Freelove (5.11b) * This short novelty route climbs the summit cap of Lunch Rock. Surprisingly exposed and exciting. From the bolt anchor of *No Free Lunches,* traverse right on a ledge, mantle the lip of an overhang at a bolt, then climb the delicate face past a bolt to the top. **Pro:** CDs from 1 to 3 inches for the anchor. **FA:** Bart Barry, et al., 1993.

Lunch Rock

Flintstone Slab

Fingertrip

FLINTSTONE SLAB

This wonderfully featured, high-angle slab hosts a collection of some of the best face climbs on Tahquitz, combining a mix of edges, friction, and thin flakes, all on excellent-quality rock. It is positioned directly above and right of Lunch Rock, framed by the flakes of *Human Fright* on the left and the arches of *Fingertrip* on the right. The face is in the shade in the morning and gets sun in the afternoon. There are numerous rappel descents from bolt anchors, described in the route descriptions and on the topos.

1. Mr. Slate (5.10d) ** This route climbs through a section of very high-quality rock on incut edges. Be fore-warned: There is a huge runout on 5.7 face climbing at the top of the pitch. Climb a short distance up the *Human Fright* dihedral, then traverse right to the first bolt. After clipping the first bolt, it is advisable to climb back and remove the pro from *Human Fright* to prevent rope drag higher. Climb past six bolts on fairly sustained, slightly runout 5.10 face climbing, then run it out (5.7 R) up to a ledge with a 2-bolt belay/rappel anchor. You can

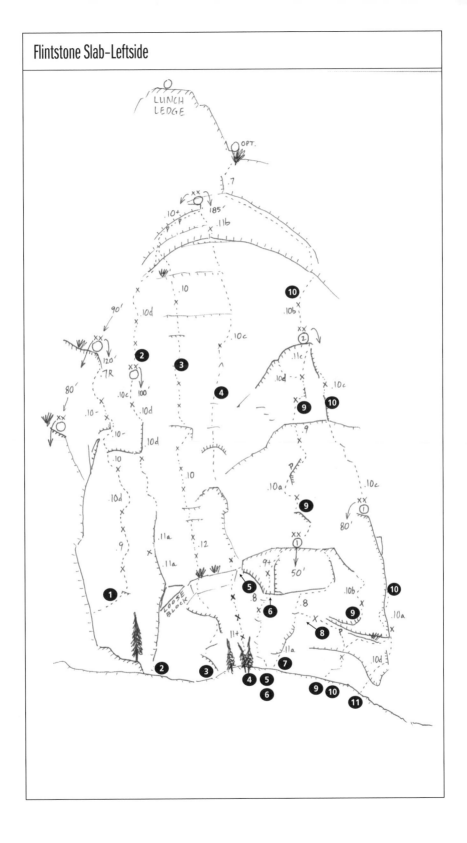

place pro between the fourth and fifth bolts. **Descent:** Rappel 120 feet or, with one rope, rap 80 feet to the *Human Fright* anchor, then 80 feet to the ground. **Pro:** a few 1- to 2-inch CDs. **FA:** Bob Gaines and Charlie Peterson, August 1996.

2. Fred (5.11a) *** Fantastic face climbing up a very smooth section of impeccable rock, except for a scary loose block near the start. The first pitch is most popular, the second pitch less so. **Pitch 1:** Begin just right of a large pine tree, almost directly above Lunch Rock. Climb a corner past the loose block, then up a tricky move (5.11a, thin gear) to a bolt. Step right to a flake, then climb up to a bolt. Move right and up a tiny right-facing corner (5.10d), then step left and climb (5.10c) to a third bolt, then up (5.10d) to a 3-bolt anchor (100 feet). **Pitch 2:** Climb the white slab past three bolts (5.10d), then for a super finish, climb the top section of *The Great Gazoo* up to its bolt anchor. **Descent:** Rap 90 feet to the *Fred* anchor or 185 feet to the ground. **Pro:** very thin nuts, TCUs and CDs from 0.3 to 0.75 inch for pitch 1, a few to 2 inches for pitch 2. **FA:** Charles Cole and Randy Vogel, 1981.

3. The Great Gazoo (5.12b) ** A long pitch up gorgeous rock with a stand-out crux. Begin right of *Fred* and climb up through flakes to a block with mountain mahogany. Crank past two

bolts up a crux blank section that is both delicate and powerful. Climb the face above past six bolts up to roofs, where two fixed pins protect the final (5.10+) moves up a right-leaning flake to a 2-bolt anchor. **Descent:** Rap 90 feet to the *Fred* anchor or 185 feet to the ground. **Pro:** 0.5- to 2-inch CDs. **FA:** Tony Sartin and Tom Murphy, September 2007.

4. Twinkle Toes (5.11d) * Start just left of *Switchbacks Direct,* where three pine trees grow close together at the base of the cliff. Climb a short distance up a pine tree to clip the first bolt. Climb past two more bolts (5.11d) up to a block/ledge and a fourth bolt. Continue up flakes past a small, distinctive black arch easily seen from below, then up and slightly right for about 40 feet to a bolt. Go up and right (5.10c) from the bolt, then up a runout slab (5.8 R) to an over-hang where a bolt protects a tricky move (5.11b) up to a 2-bolt anchor. For an easier start you can climb *Switchbacks Direct* (5.8). **Descent:** Rappel 90 feet to the *Fred* anchor or 185 feet to the ground. **Pro:** to 3 inches. **FA:** Tom Murphy and Tony Sartin, September 2008.

5. Switchbacks Direct (5.8) Same start as *Betty.* Climb the face up to a bolt, then move left and up a curving left-facing flake. **Pro:** to 2.5 inches. **FA:** Dave Rearick, 1958.

6. Betty (5.9+) * Short and sweet. From the bolt on *Switchbacks Direct*, continue straight up to another bolt that protects a tricky move up to a two-bolt anchor at a small ledge (50 feet). **Pro:** 1.75-inch CD below the second bolt. **FA:** Yvonne Gaines and Bob Gaines, July 4, 1994.

7. Barney (5.11a TR) From the *Betty* anchor you can toprope the curving thin flake just right of *Betty*. **FA:** Bob Gaines, July 4, 1994.

8. Dino (5.10c) From the first bolt at the start of *Blanketty Blank,* move up left to a fixed pin, then traverse straight left past a bolt (5.10c), then up to a horizontal crack. Move right, then up to the 2-bolt anchor shared with *Betty* (50 feet). **Pro:** CDs from 0.75 to 1.5 inches. **FA:** Bob Gaines and Bob Carmichael, July 1994.

9. The Quarry (5.11c or 5.10d) **
A meandering, slightly runout two-pitch face climb with good pro at the tough spots. From the last bolt you can move left for an easier (5.10d) finish. **Pitch 1:** At the first bolt on *Blanketty Blank,* move up and left to a fixed pin, then over a bulge to a bolt. Slippery 5.10 face climbing leads to a 2-bolt belay at a small ledge. **Pitch 2:** Weave more or less straight up the face above past four bolts and a fixed pin, with the crux above the last bolt, to the 2-bolt anchor shared with *Blanketty Blank*. **Descent:** Two 80-foot rappels to the ground (or one 165-foot rappel). **Pro:** several CDs from 0.75 to 2 inches. **FA:** Bob Gaines and Mike Borrello, October 1993.

10. Blanketty Blank (5.10c PG) **
Thoughtful face climbing with many of the hard moves protected by thin nuts. Start about 40 feet downhill and right of *Betty* at a bolt beneath a small arch. **Pitch 1:** Climb past the bolt (height-dependent 5.9+) up and right to an overhang, then traverse right around the corner to a bolt. At the start of the corner, climb the arête on the left (5.10a), then follow the right-facing corner up to a 2-bolt belay/rappel anchor (80 feet). **Pitch 2:** A tough move (5.10c) right above the belay leads to easier climbing and a ledge at the base of a tiny left-facing corner. At this point you can either angle left (5.6) on face climbing to a flake that diagonals back up and right to the anchor, or go straight up the tiny corner to face climbing (5.10c) past a bolt, then follow another tiny left-facing corner up to the 2-bolt belay/rappel anchor. From here you can descend in two rappels (80 feet) or rappel 165 feet to the ground. **Pitch 3:** (5.10b) Climb past a bolt on a slab, moving up and right to join *Fingertrip* for its third pitch. **Pro:** several thin to 1 inch for pitches 1 and 2, standard rack to continue. **FA:** Tom Frost and Harry Daley, June 1959. **FFA:** Bob Kamps and Tom Higgins, 1963. **FA pitch**

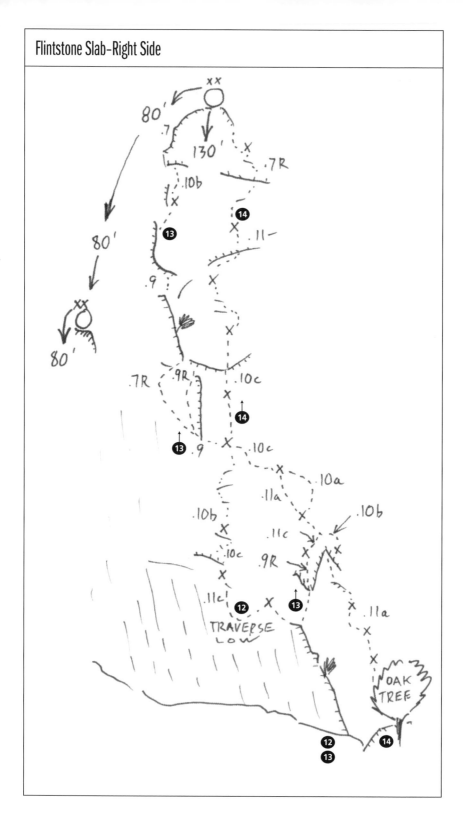

3: John Long and others, 1977. **FA pitch 2 direct:** Randy Vogel and Paul Schweizer, 1984.

11. Blanketty Blank Direct Start (5.10d) Start 15 feet downhill and right of *Blanketty Blank* and climb up, then right, past a small flake to join *Blanketty Blank* just before its right-facing dihedral. **Pro:** thin nuts, CDs from 0.75 to 1 inch. **FA:** Bob Gaines and Bob Carmichael, July 1994.

12. Pebbles (5.11c) ** Start about 50 feet down and right from *Blanketty Blank* at a small right-facing corner. Climb the corner (1-inch pro) up to a bolt, then traverse down and left, then up (5.11c) to a second bolt. Face climbing (5.10) past another bolt leads to a fourth bolt (shared with *Wilma* and *Bedrock*). Move left to finish up *Wilma*, or continue straight up and finish on *Bedrock*. **Descent:** Rappel 80 feet to the *Blanketty Blank* anchor or 130 feet to the ground. **Pro:** thin to 1.5 inches. **FA:** Bob Gaines, August 1994.

13. Wilma (5.11c R/X) * Never popular due to a serious 5.9 runout at the start, the upper section is quite good and makes for a less scary route (albeit with some mandatory 5.7 R) when combined with *Pebbles* to start. Start about 50 feet down

and right from *Blanketty Blank* at a small right-facing corner. Climb the corner (1-inch pro), then climb up to and over a flake (5.9 R/X) to a bolt that protects the crux (5.11c). Climb up past two more bolts, then traverse left past a fourth bolt over to a right-facing corner. Follow this intermittent flake/corner until it peters out, where a bolt protects moves (5.10b) up to a flake that leads to the 2-bolt anchor shared with *Bedrock*. **Descent:** Rappel 80 feet to the *Blanketty Blank* anchor or 130 feet to the ground. **Pro:** to 2 inches.

14. Bedrock (5.11a) ** 160 feet of sustained face climbing on exquisite rock. Begin on the far right side of Flintstone Slab, downhill from *Blanketty Blank*, where a large oak tree grows close to the wall. Climb incut edges (5.11-) past three bolts up to an overlapping arch. At the fourth bolt, move up left to join *Wilma* for three bolts, then at the seventh bolt climb straight up, where five more bolts lead to a 2-bolt belay/rappel anchor. Judicious deployment of slings is necessary to reduce rope drag. **Descent:** With one rope you can rappel 80 feet to the *Blanketty Blank* anchor, then less than 80 feet to the ground. **Pro:** twelve quickdraws, slings. **FA:** Bob Gaines, Todd Gordon, and Charlie Peterson, August 1997.

WEST FACE—RIGHT SIDE

Viewed from Lunch Rock, this is the sector of the cliff to the right of Flintstone Slab, extending all the way to the great arête of *The Edge* on the far right. From Lunch Rock, walk straight right on a rough trail until it climbs up to the base of the cliff. *The Slab, Crimes of Passion,* and *Fingertrip* are found here. The remaining routes are found by walking farther right to where the trail intersects the base of the cliff and goes uphill a short distance to *The Edge,* which is on the prominent arête that marks the right border of the West Face. Continuing around the corner to the right of *The Edge* takes you to the South Face.

Descent: For routes that go to the top, descend via the Friction Route. For routes that end part way up the cliff, rappel descents are listed in the route descriptions.

1. The Slab (5.9-) * This route is sometimes mistaken for *Fingertrip,* much to the regret of those climbers, who usually get spanked, as it's much harder, with some tough jamming. Climb the left-facing dihedral up the left side of the prominent, white exfoliation slab clearly visible from Lunch Rock. Near the top, exit up a hand crack that diagonals right on the outside face of the slab. **Pro:** to 3 inches. **FA:** Harry Daley and D. McCelland, August 1958. **FFA:** Bob Kamps and TM Herbert, 1963.

2. Point Blank (5.12b) * Another Tahquitz arête testpiece on excellent

West Face—Right Side

rock. Climb about 40 feet up *The Slab,* make a delicate step right (5.10 R) to a shelf, then bear-hug, smear, and palm your way up the blunt "arête" past six bolts (5.12b) to a crack (1.5-inch CD) that diagonals right up to a 2-bolt anchor. **Pro:** to 3 inches. For a great (and less harrowing) start, clip the first three bolts of *Crimes of Passion Direct,* then move left to the first bolt on *Point Blank* (nine bolts total). **Descent:** Rappel 110 feet. **Pro:** to 3 inches. **FA:** Bob Gaines, May 1998.

3. Crimes of Passion Direct (5.11d) ** For an easier (5.10d) and classic face climb, climb the first two pitches of this route and finish up *Fingertrip.* **Pitch 1:** Begin with the start of *The Slab,* then move right to a spike of rock you can sling with a runner. Climb up to two difficult (5.10) mantle shelves, both protected by bolts, then friction and crimp up a clean, white slab past three bolts (5.10d) to a narrow ledge with a 2-bolt anchor. You can rappel from here with a 70-meter rope (110 feet). **Pitch 2:** Climb up and left past four bolts on a beautiful slab, then back right to a fourth bolt (5.10b). Climb up to *Fingertrip* (optional belay here) and cross that route, climbing up into a smaller left-facing dihedral just right of the huge *Fingertrip* arch. Jam up the dihedral (5.8) to a bolt, then move right and up (5.11d) on a very thin slab to *Fingertip Traverse*'s namesake leftward traverse.

Pro: to 4 inches. **FA:** Bob Gaines and Yvonne Gaines, August 1987.

4. Fingertrip (5.7) *** From Lunch Rock, walk right along the trail until it meets the base of the rock. The first pitch begins just up and left from this point, starting in a left-facing corner directly behind a huge (5-foot diameter) pine tree. **Pitch 1:** Lieback and stem up the dihedral (5.7). At the top, either continue straight up the corner via fingertip liebacking (5.8-) to a belay at a small ledge with a large pine tree, or jam the splitter crack (5.6) that diagonals up and left, then move back to the pine tree belay (165 feet). **Pitch 2:** Lieback past blocks to a vertical crack system; follow this for about 40 feet, then traverse left across a smooth slab, around the corner and into the big arch (which is a big left-facing dihedral at this point), and climb up to a semi-hanging belay about 40 feet higher under the arch. **Pitch 3:** Climb up cracks for about 20 feet, undercling 30 feet left under another arch, then power through the overhang (5.7) at the apex of the arch to a small ledge with a huge mountain mahogany about 20 feet higher. You can belay here if you want to closely watch your second, or climb easy face (5.0) to reach Lunch Ledge about 50 feet higher and belay there. **Pro:** to 3 inches. **FA:** Chuck Wilts, Don Gillespie, and Jerry Rosenblatt, September 1946.

5. Fingertip Traverse (5.5) ** (See topo on page 125.) From Lunch Rock, walk right on the trail for about 200 feet to where it climbs up to the base of the rock. (You'll be near the base of the *Fingertrip* route.) From here, walk right to just past the point where the trail begins going uphill. **Pitch 1:** Climb a low-angle, 4th-class gully, moving left at the top to ledges with two oak trees growing close together. Belay at the first oak tree (60 feet). **Pitch 2:** Climb the upper oak tree until you can move left, face climbing around the corner, just below an overhang, then climb a crack to a large, bushy ledge known as "Jungle Ledge" (50 feet). **Pitch 3:** Lieback a tricky right-facing corner (5.5), then face climb up and left to a small belay stance (60 feet) (0.5- to 2-inch gear anchor). **Pitch 4:** Continue up and left to two fixed pins that mark the start of the route's namesake "fingertip traverse." Hand traverse diagonally up and left (5.3) with intense exposure (taking care to protect your follower) to easier (5.0) climbing up a crack system that leads to Lunch Ledge. There is an optional belay at a huge mountain mahogany at the end of the traverse. Follow *Angel's Fright* above Lunch Ledge. **Pro:** to 2.5 inches. **FA:** Jim Smith, Bob Brinton, Arthur Johnson, and William Rice, September 1936.

6. Dos Equis Direct (5.11a) * Start about 40 feet up the 4th-class *Fingertip Traverse* gully at a ledge. **Pitch 1:** Climb a flake out right, then up to a thin crack with a bolt (5.8), moving right on a ramp to a second bolt that protects thin slab moves (5.10c) up to the third bolt on the second pitch of *El Camino Real*. Belay at a tree on Jungle Ledge. **Pitch 2:** From the extreme right edge of Jungle Ledge, crank a short, steep section past two bolts

West Face—Right Side

onto the outside face of the slab, then up easier face climbing past two bolts. A fifth bolt protects thin (5.10c) and slightly runout face moves up to a crack that leads to a 2-bolt belay/rappel anchor. **Descent:** Rappel 100 feet to Jungle Ledge, then rappel 100 feet from a tree plus some 4th-class downclimbing to the ground. **Pro:** several thin to 2 inches. **FA:** Bob Gaines and Ann Albert, June 1986. **FA direct:** Bob Gaines and Frank Bentwood, 2010.

7. El Camino Real (5.10a) ** The third pitch is one of the great lieback cracks of Idyllwild. Begin a short distance uphill from *Fingertip Traverse*. The start is at a ledge with a huge pine tree (the largest tree growing above the trail), accessed by scrambling about 15 feet up a smooth groove. **Pitch 1:** (5.10-) Start just behind the tree. Bouldery moves at an incipient crack (5.10a) lead to an overhang. Climb over the roof to a bolt on the right, then up a thin face (5.10a/b), working up and left to easy cracks leading to a belay at blocks. Most climbers traverse left under the overhang, then up to the belay, for an easier variation. **Pitch 2:** Climb past two bolts on an arête (5.9), then make a friction traverse left and up past another bolt to a belay at a tree on Jungle Ledge. **Pitch 3:** Lieback the awesome left-facing dihedral on the right to a ledge with a 2-bolt belay/rappel anchor. To descend from here, rappel 100 feet to Jungle Ledge, then rappel 100 feet from an oak tree

plus some 4th-class downclimbing to the ground. **Pitch 4:** Up and left on 5.8 cracks, then traverse right to join *Jensen's Jaunt*. **Pro:** several thin to 3 inches. **FA:** Royal Robbins, Harry Daley, and Janie Taylor, November 1961.

8. Desperado (5.10d) TR * From the *El Camino Real* bolt anchor on pitch 3, you can toprope the steep slab left of the corner. **FA:** Bob Gaines and Dave Cherney, June 2003.

9. Coffin Nail (5.8) ** The crux pitch is one of the best 5.8 cracks on Tahquitz, with sheer architecture and great jamming and liebacking. **Pitch 1:** Begin from the *El Camino Real* starting ledge and climb up and right past trees onto a face to a move (5.6) up to grab a mountain mahogany, then up to a belay at a pine tree in a gully. **Pitch 2:** Climb a rather unprotected chimney (5.6), then exit left onto a belay ledge. **Pitch 3:** Up the chimney to blocks, then move left onto the face to avoid them. Lieback a steepening crack, then hand jam a flaring crack (5.8), above which the angle lessens and the crack thins to finger width and leads to a rest spot at a little ledge on the left. Lieback up the corner (3-inch CD) to a small roof, then power over this on finger jams to easier crack climbing up to a belay on *Jensen's Jaunt*. (Pitches 2 and 3 can be combined, but you'll get severe rope drag.) **Pro:** thin to 3 inches, including several each from 1 to 3 inches. **FA:** Unknown.

10. On the Road (5.10c) ** Begin with the start of *Jensen's Jaunt,* then climb up and left to the base of a long flake system that turns into a clean left-facing dihedral. Lieback the corner until you can exit right to *Jensen's Jaunt.* **Pro:** several thin to 2 inches. **FA:** Unknown.

11. Jensen's Jaunt (5.6) ** One of the early classics, this moderate route begins at the southwest corner of the rock, just left of the massive arête of *The Edge.* Start from a ledge with trees about 20 feet above the trail. **Pitch 1:** Climb a short pitch up easy, blocky terrain to a nice belay ledge just right of small oak tree, below the start of the more difficult climbing (70 feet). **Pitch 2:** Climb a steeper section with thin cracks, then move up and right and jam a long left-leaning crack to a belay stance about 30 feet below the overhangs. The *Traitor Horn* route traverses right from just above this belay (180 feet). **Pitch 3:** Continue up the crack around the left side of the overhangs to an exposed and awkward

West Face—Right Side

move where the crack widens (3- to 4-inch CD useful). Follow cracks up to a nice ledge (optional belay here with 2- to 3-inch CDs), then climb up to a belay at a sprawling tree (150 feet). **Pitches 4 and 5:** The normal finish climbs up and right to a blocky ledge at the base of the broad shoulder forming the southwest corner of the rock, then up an easy (5.2) friction slab to the top. For a more challenging direct finish, continue up the massive left-facing, arching corner (5.7) and belay just beneath the summit headwall, finishing by moving down and left around the corner to avoid the headwall (exposed 4th class), then up to the top. **Pro:** to 4 inches. **FA:** Carl Jensen, Jim Smith, and Don McDonald, August 1938.

12. The Hangover (5.13a) * Like a boulder problem in the sky, this route blasts through the massive overhang just right of where *Jensen's Jaunt* avoids the overhang on the left. From the second belay of *Jensen's Jaunt,* climb up and right into a steep left-facing corner, then move left and tackle the overhang at a bolt. A massive dynamic move is required. Belay about 40 feet higher. **Pro:** to 3 inches. **FA:** (A3) Royal Robbins, Jerry Gallwas, Frank Martin, and Mike Sherrick, August 1954. **FFA:** John Long, Rick Accomazzo, Rob Muir, and Mike Lechlinski, 1978.

13. The Acrobat (5.11b) ** Wildly gymnastic climbing up the overhanging arête and roof left of *Pearly Gate.* From the tiny belay stance at the base of the alcove, fire up past a bolt on the overhanging arête, clip the second bolt, make a big, height-dependent reach (or dyno!) out left, then go up and right past a bolt to a roof. Clip the fourth bolt with a long

West Face—Right Side

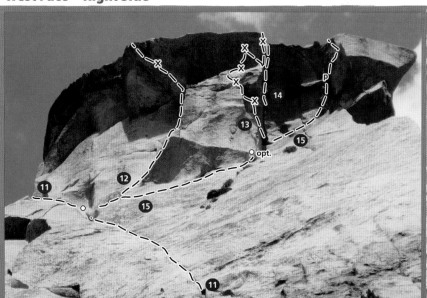

sling to prevent rope drag, then climb down and right a few feet around the arête, then back up to a left knee lock that facilitates clipping the fifth bolt. Above the overhang a long sling is useful to tie off a knob. Belay about 50 feet above the roof at a block with a mountain mahogany. **Pro:** to 2.5 inches. **FA:** Bob Gaines and Frank Bentwood, August 2007.

14. Pearly Gate (5.10a) ** From the belay on *Traitor Horn,* climb straight up through the left side of the alcove and lieback a short overhanging crack with a tricky exit, belaying about 40 feet higher at a block. **Pro:** several CDs to 4 inches. **FA:** Dave Rearick and Bob Kamps, 1969.

15. Traitor Horn (5.8) *** Intimidating for the grade, with a spectacular, exposed crux. Start with the first two pitches of *Jensen's Jaunt,* to the belay just below the overhangs. **Pitch 3:** Traverse down low, on a slab between flakes (5.8) beneath a protruding horn of rock. This is the "traitor horn," as the "true horn" can now be seen farther up and right as a pointed block that juts out. Traverse right to the start of the corner leading to the *Pearly Gate* crack (optional belay stance here) and climb up to the upper right corner of the alcove to fixed pins. A big reach gets you over to, then onto the "true horn" and one of the most exposed perches on Tahquitz. Move a few feet left, over the bulge, then belay about 30 feet higher (1- to 3-inch gear). A

long pitch up an easy (5.0) but runout low-angle slab gets you to the top. **Pro:** thin to 3 inches. **FA:** Jim Smith, Arthur Johnson, and M. Holton, August 1938. **FFA:** Roy Gorin and William Shand, 1941.

16. The Edge (5.11b R) *** This psychological testpiece climbs the stunning arête dividing the West and South Faces. **Pitch 1:** Climb *Jenson's Jaunt* to a belay in an alcove at the base of the long, left-diagonalling crack. **Pitch 2:** Traverse out right past two bolts (5.11b after the second bolt) over to the "edge," where a third bolt protects a 5.10d move, followed by a *long* runout (5.10a R) to a fourth bolt that protects a final 5.10 section up to the sanctuary of a 2-bolt anchor. **Pitch 3:** Bust a 5.10d move above the belay, then step left and climb a crack up to *Traitor Horn.* Climbing directly up the arête instead of stepping left is even more challenging (5.11b R). Finish on *Traitor Horn.* **Pro:** thin to 3 inches. **FA:** Tobin Sorenson and Gib Lewis, 1976.

17. Turbo Flange (5.11c R) *** Perhaps the most prominent line on Tahquitz, and one of the boldest leads on the rock. This direct start to *The Edge* climbs directly from the base of the arête's left side. Climb up to a bolt (5.8), then crank a hard slab move (5.11c) followed by easier but runout slab moves (5.11a R) up to where *The Edge* traverses over from *Jensen's Jaunt* at its third bolt. **Pro:** to 3 inches. **FA:** John Long and Dwight Brooks, 1984.

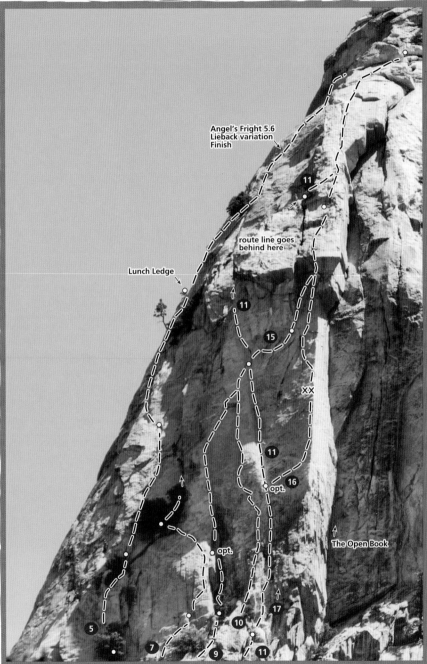

Angel's Fright 5.6
Lieback variation
Finish

11

route line goes
behind here

Lunch Ledge

11

15

XX

11

16

opt.

The Open Book

opt.

17

5

10

7

9   11

South Face Overview

West Face Bulge

Friction Route
Descent

Right
Side

Center

West Face

Open Book
Area

Left Wall
Area

To Lunch
Rock

Trail

8.

South Face

The South Face comprises the entire section of Tahquitz to the right of *The Edge,* which is on the prominent southwest arête forming the definitive border between the West Face and South Face of Tahquitz Rock. *The Open Book* climbs the crack in the huge dihedral just to the right of *The Edge.* These distinctive features can be seen from miles away. The South Face is not as tall as other sections of the rock—roughly 300 feet high—but the rock quality is excellent, featuring some of the best granite on the planet.

The best climbing conditions here are during cooler weather, as this south-facing cliff bakes in the sun during most of the day and is uncomfortably hot during the dog days of summer. *The Open Book* is in the shade in the early morning and late afternoon.

Approach: From Lunch Rock, walk right on a rough trail that climbs up to the base of the southwest corner of the rock. Continue right, staying very close to the base of the rock, around the corner, and the South Face will come into view.

Descent: For all routes that go to the top of the South Face, the standard descent route is to scramble down the Friction Route.

Rappel Descents: A rappel descent can be made with two 165-foot rappels beginning from bolts near the top of *The Open Book* to the bolt anchor on *Green Arch,* then to the ground. The second rappel is overhanging, and you'll be free hanging for the bottom half.

With a 70-meter rope you can descend in three rappels from *The Open Book* bolt anchor. The first rappel (35 meters, 115 feet) takes you to the *Green Arch*'s 2-bolt anchor. From here, rappel to *Mavericks*'s first- or second-pitch anchor (hanging stances, 35 meters to the first-pitch anchor). From either anchor it's less than 100 feet to the ground. The last rappel is free hanging for some distance.

From the top of *Left Ski Track* you can descend in three 100-foot rappels, the first from a pine tree (slings may or may not be in place) to *The Heathen*'s third-pitch bolt anchor (good ledge), the second to the bolt anchor on *Left Ski Track* (good ledge), and the third to the ground. *Caution:* The last rappel barely reaches with a 60-meter rope (a bit of downclimbing is

South Face Rappels

required) and is best with a 70-meter rope (35 meters or 115 feet).

Note: While these rappels may seem convenient, they are time-consuming and complicated. It is quicker and far easier for most climbers to descend via the Friction Route.

LEFT WALL AREA

This steep wall is at the base of the left side of *The Open Book* dihedral, featuring one- and two-pitch face climbs on exquisite rock. In the summer it gets shade in the late afternoon, after about 2:30 p.m.

Descent: All these routes have bolted rappel anchors (less than 100 feet).

1. Bibliography (5.10b PG/R) * Start about 50 feet downhill and left of *Open Book*. Reach left to a flake, stem up a shallow, difficult-to-protect corner (5.10-), exit left to an arête, then up slabby (5.8), somewhat runout face climbing up and right to a 2-bolt belay at a nice ledge. **Pro:** thin nuts and CDs to 1 inch. **FA:** Bob Gaines, John Rosholt, Sheryl Basye, Mark Hoffman, June 1994.

2. The Glossary (5.11b) * Start just right of *Bibliography*. Jam a short crack that diagonals left, stem up a slick corner, then power over the bulge on the right to the 2-bolt belay shared with *Bibliography*. **FA:** Bob Gaines, Mark Hoffman, and John Rosholt, June 1994.

3. The Bookend (5.11a) ** This pitch is located just right of the huge arête of *The Edge,* starting at the 2-bolt belay 60 feet up. Climb a shallow corner up and right past four bolts to a thin crack. A 1-inch CD is very useful to protect the final step-up to the belay. **Pro:** 1-inch CD. **FA:** Bob Gaines and Charlie Peterson, July 1994.

4. Hedgehog (5.11d) * Crank your way up the steep wall between *The Glossary* and *The Hedge* past five bolts. A small overhang at the third bolt is the crux. **FA:** Bob Gaines and John Rosholt, June 1994.

John Rosholt was a talented climber who accompanied me on several first ascents on the Left Wall. Nicknamed "the gambler," John lived a peripatetic climber's lifestyle financed by his earnings as a professional gambler and card shark in Las Vegas. John disappeared in January 2005, his whereabouts unknown. His car was found four months later in the parking lot of the Silverton casino in Vegas. His remains were found five years later up at the Red Rocks, in Black Velvet Canyon, near the base of the *Prince of Darkness* route. The cause of his death remains a mystery.

XX
80'
5.11a
1 inch
CD
5.10d
❸
5.10b
5.10c
5.12c
❸
5.10b
XX
60'
5.8 PG/R
5.10a
5.8
❷
5.10a
The Open Book
5.10b
5.11c
5.11b
5.11d
5.11a
P
5.11d
5.10a
5.10d
5.10b
❺ ❻
4
❶ ❷

5. The Hedge (5.10d) * Begin about 30 feet downhill and left of *The Open Book*. A bolt protects a powerful reach left (5.10d) to a flake. Undercling left, then lieback a vertical crack for about 20 feet until you can move left (5.10a) across the face to a two-bolt belay stance. **Pro:** nuts and CDs from 0.5 to 1.5 inches. **FA:** Gib Lewis and Charles Cole, 1983.

6. Bookworm (5.12c) ** Clip the first bolt of *The Hedge* and climb directly up over the small roof (5.11d, 1.5-inch CD) to a fixed pin. Climb past a bolt on very thin edges (5.11+, stay right) up to a small ledge. From here five more bolts protect tricky face moves on the slightly overhanging wall. A 1-inch CD can be placed in the thin crack above the last bolt. **FA:** Bob Gaines, July 1994.

THE OPEN BOOK AREA

This area includes Tahquitz's most prominent dihedral, *The Open Book*, and includes the routes immediately to the right of the corner. It gets shade in the early morning, then is in the sun until very late in the afternoon.

1. The Open Book (5.9) *** America's first 5.9. This route follows the enormous right-facing dihedral that can be seen from miles away. **Pitch 1:** (5.9) Climb a 3rd-class ramp for about 40 feet, and up a short, slightly overhanging face (5.8), then traverse left over to the main crack in the corner. Climb the corner up to the crux—jamming, liebacking, and

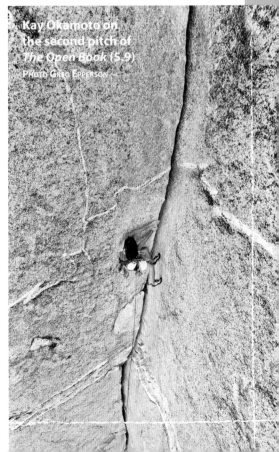

Kay Okamoto on the second pitch of *The Open Book* (5.9)
PHOTO GREG EPPERSON

stemming up to a gaping flake, then climb a short chimney up to a belay in an alcove at a tiny ledge (cramped for a party of three). **Pitch 2:** Stem, lieback, and jam the widening crack in the grand dihedral (5.9, 3- to 4-inch CDs useful) up to the overhang (optional belay here, but it's awkward and cramped), then move right, turning the overhang, and belaying at a small stance with tiny, sloping ledges about 20 feet higher (1.5- to 2.5-inch CDs critical). **Pitch 3:** Lieback up the corner (now less steep) (5.2), stem and climb past a huge chockstone (5.4), and where the crack turns into a wide chimney, move right onto an easy but unprotected friction slab (5.6 R), moving farther right and through a short overhang at a slot/chimney (3-inch CD). Follow this crack (which becomes low angle) to a 2-bolt belay about 30 feet higher. (The rappel descent route begins here.) **Pitch 4:** Stroll up an exposed but easy (4th-class) ramp to the top (40 feet). **Pro:** thin to 4 inches, including several from 3 to 4 inches. **FA:** (5.8, A2, using 2 x 4 wooden pitons!) John Mendenhall and Harry Sutherland, September 1947. **FFA:** Royal Robbins and Don Wilson, 1952.

2. Zig Zag (5.10b) ** **Pitch 1:** Climb the overhang at the start of *The Open Book,* traverse right to a bolt, then climb a delicate face (5.9) straight up to a spectacular lieback flake just left of *Mechanic's Route.* Belay where the flake eventually merges into

> When John Mendenhall and Harry Sutherland first climbed *The Open Book* in 1947, there were no pitons available that were wide enough to fit much of the crack, so they improvised and hammered in wooden pitons they had crafted from two-by-fours to use for direct aid, in some instances standing on the two-by-fours like rungs on a ladder. When a young Royal Robbins free climbed the entire route in 1952, it became America's first route to receive the 5.9 rating.

Mechanic's Route. **Pitch 2:** (5.10b) Follow the vertical crack (*Mechanic's Route* moves right onto the face after about 30 feet) through a small overhang onto a slab, where the crack becomes very thin and eventually peters out, then either move left to finish on *The Open Book* or traverse right to finish on *Mechanic's Route.* **Pro:** to 4 inches. **FA:** TM Herbert and Mark Powell, 1961. **FFA:** Mark Powell and Bob Kamps, 1967.

3. Flashback (5.10d) ** This two-pitch variation begins after the first pitch of *The Open Book.* **Pitch 1:** Lieback the obvious arch that diagonals up and right (5.10-), then continue right with face moves up to the belay shared with *Zig Zag* and *Mechanic's Route.*

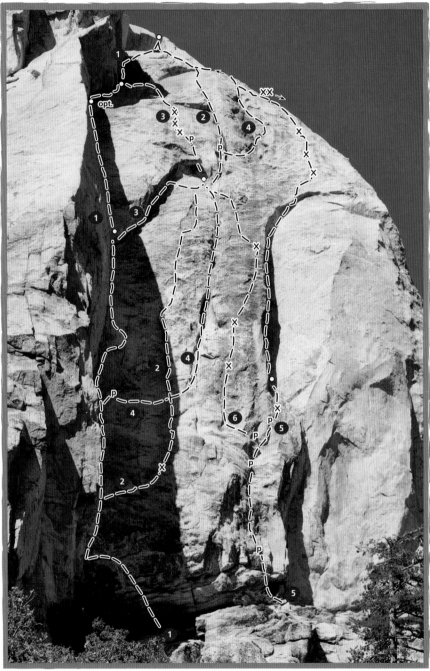

Pitch 2: Mantle onto the overhanging block on the left (5.10b), climb a thin corner, step up to a fixed pin, then crimp up a steep slab past three bolts (5.10d), moving left to the belay on *The Open Book* (2- to 2.5-inch CDs). **Pro:** many thin to one 4-inch CD. **FA:** Bob Gaines and Tommy Romero, August 1995.

4. Mechanic's Route (5.8 PG/R) *** One of America's boldest face climbs in 1937, led in sneakers with a manila rope! **Pitch 1:** Climb the first section of the *The Open Book* to just below its crux, clip a fixed pin, then traverse 20 feet right to a knobby crack that widens into a chimney; belay just above it (gear anchor, #2 camalot useful). **Pitch 2:** Climb about 30 feet up a crack, then move right onto a committing face and climb up and right through big, rounded buckets (5.8 PG/R), then move slightly left up to a 5.6 crack. A bit higher you can traverse right to the two-bolt belay at a nice ledge on *Green Arch*. You can rappel from here with two ropes (165 feet) to the ground, or with one 60-meter rope you can rappel to *Mavericks's* second-pitch anchor (hanging stance), then 100 feet to the ground. The last rappel is free hanging for some distance. **Pitch 3:** Up and right up a huge corner (5.5) takes you to the top. **Pro:** thin to 3 inches. **FA:** Dick Jones and Glen Dawson, October 1937.

5. Green Arch (5.11c) *** Aesthetic and challenging. This route face climbs up to, then follows the narrow dihedral just right of *Mechanic's Route*. The second pitch is one of the great leads on Tahquitz. The difficulty of an on-sight lead is hugely dependent on the number of fixed pins in place. In the last twenty years I've seen as many as ten and as few as five. Without the pins you can fiddle in thin gear, but it definitely adds to the pump factor. **Pitch 1:** Climb up over a small overhang, then face climb to a little corner that slants up and right. Fixed pins and a bolt protect face climbing (5.10a) up a small ledge (gear anchor, 0.3-inch CD, stoppers #4, #6, #9) at the base of the dihedral. **Pitch 2:** Stem and chimney up the dihedral (5.11b, usually with many fixed pins) to a possible rest stance on the left before the arch curves right. Where the arch curves to horizontal, climb up over it (5.11c), moving right to a bolt, then up the slab past two more bolts to a good ledge with a 2-bolt belay/rappel anchor. From here you can rappel to the ground with two ropes (165 feet) or make two less than 100-foot rappels to the bolt anchor (hanging stance) on *Mavericks's* second pitch. With a 70-meter rope you can rappel to the bolt anchor on *Mavericks's* first pitch (35 meters, 115 feet) by swinging over to the right. **Pitch 3:** A 5.5 corner/crack system on the right leads to the top. **Pro:** many thin to medium nuts,

CDs from 0.3 to 1.5 inches. **FA:** (5.8, A2) Mark and Beverly Powell, 1964. **FFA:** Rick Accomazzo, John Long, and Tobin Sorenson, 1975.

6. Torque Wrench (5.10d) ** On the first pitch of *Green Arch,* after the right-slanting corner, climb up and left to an arête with three bolts (5.10d) , then go up and left on easier but runout (5.8), knobby face climbing to the *Mechanic's Route* belay. **Pro:** to 3 inches. **FA:** Kevin Powell and Darrell Hensel, July 1993.

SOUTH FACE—CENTER

The following climbs are located on the center of the South Face, to the right of and around the corner from the huge dihedral of *The Open Book.*

This is a very hot place in the summer, as it does not receive any shade until very late in the day.

Approach: Follow the trail past the point where you can see the twin curving cracks of the "ski tracks" that split the center of the wall, then cut back left to a large pine tree at the base of the "ski tracks."

1. Mavericks (5.11d) *** The first pitch is a well-protected direct start to an old route called *New Wave* (5.12 R) that traverses in from the right (with groundfall potential at its crux). **Pitch 1:** (5.11d, 4 bolts) Power over the overhang (5.11b), then make a delicate traverse left (5.11d) on thin slab moves to a hanging belay at a 2-bolt belay/rappel anchor. **Pitch 2:** Up past

South Face—Center Overview

two bolts, then tiptoe left (5.11b) to a third bolt and easier (5.10a) face climbing up to a 2-bolt anchor. **Pitch 2 variation:** You can also traverse left from the belay over to the first pitch of *Flying Circus,* climbing past two bolts (5.11d) up to the anchor. The lower section of *Flying Circus's* first pitch is rarely climbed (5.10 A4). Rappel from here (100 feet to the ground) or continue up *Flying Circus*. **FA New Wave:** Gib Lewis and Charles Cole, 1983. **FA Mavericks, pitch 1:** (TR) Dave Mayville and Bob Gaines, July 1999. **First lead, Mavericks, pitch 1:** Bob Gaines and Frank Bentwood, August 2001. **FA Mavericks, pitch 2:** Bob Gaines and Tommy Romero, August 2005.

2. Flying Circus Pitch 2 (5.10d R) *** This pitch is the infamous "Muir Trail," named after Rob Muir, who took several 40-foot falls before completing the first ascent. From the bolt belay, climb up and right, then back left (5.10d R) to a bolt, then up and left past a second bolt on easier slab climbing to the 2-bolt belay/rappel anchor for *Green Arch*. **FA:** Rob Muir, Rick Accomazzo, and Charles Cole, August 1978.

3. The Unchaste (5.11a) ** This intimidating route begins just up and right from *Mavericks*. **Pitch 1:** Climb the left of two right-slanting cracks, then move left onto the face up to a bolt. Climb up and left (5.11a) to a flake (1.5- to 2-inch CD), then up and left past one more bolt to a nice stance at a 2-bolt

belay/rappel anchor (80-foot rappel). **Pitch 2:** Traverse down and left to a crack, then up to a shallow scoop with a bolt. From here you can traverse up and right to a second bolt (5.9, original route) or continue up and left to a different bolt (*Powell Variation,* 5.9). Both routes end at the ledge with the 2-bolt belay/rappel anchor on *Green Arch*. **Descent:** Rappel to the ground with two ropes (165 feet), or with one 60-meter rope rappel to *Mavericks's* second-pitch anchor (hanging stance), then 100 feet to the ground. The last rappel is free hanging for some distance. **FA:** (5.9, A3) Royal Robbins and Mike Sherrick, September 1957. **FFA:** Tobin Sorenson and Gib Lewis, 1974. **FA Powell Variation:** Mark and Beverly Powell, October 1964.

4. The Heathen (5.11c) ** **Pitch 1:** Climb the start of *The Chauvinist* up a short dihedral, then step left and climb a crack that leads to a spectacular face where eight bolts protect face climbing first straight up (5.11-), then left (5.10+), over to a 2-bolt belay at a small ledge in a corner above *The Unchaste* belay. **Pitch 2:** Crimp your way up a short, steep headwall of gold-colored rock past three bolts (5.11c, the third bolt is tough to clip) up to a two-bolt belay stance. **Pitch 3:** Move left (5.8) to a bolt, then go straight up the smooth slab past five more bolts (5.11a) to a big ledge with a two-bolt anchor. Two 100-foot rappels from here reach the ground (make sure you go to the bolt anchor for *Left Ski Track/Feminist* on the right, and not *The Heathen*'s anchor, which is 120 feet above the ground), or climb an easy (5.0) pitch up the corner to the top. **Pro:** to 2 inches. **FA pitches 1 and 2:** Bob Gaines and Dave Mayville, July 1999. **FA pitches 3 and 4:** Bob Gaines and Charlie Peterson, August 1999.

5. The Feminist (5.11a TR) * This is a fun toprope. Climb the start of *The Heathen* to its fourth bolt, then climb straight up through the steep "moguls" directly up to the 2-bolt belay/rappel anchor for *The Chauvinist* and *Left Ski Track* (100-foot rappel). **FA:** (TR) Bob Gaines, July 1999.

6. The Chauvinist (5.8+) ** **Pitch 1:** Start below the line of the *Left Ski Track* main crack in a short dihedral. Climb up the dihedral (5.8+), then straight up a steep, flared crack (5.8+) to easy face climbing following the left crack of *Left Ski Track,* sharing its belay. **Pitch 2:** Up a flake, then up a slab past three bolts (5.8) to a crack that leads to the leftward traverse on the last pitch of *Left Ski Track*. **Pro:** to 4 inches. **FA:** Mark Powell, T. Rygg, and Roy Coats, January 1964.

7. Left Ski Track (5.6) *** This route is found about 250 feet to the right of *The Open Book,* on a steep, featured wall split by two parallel, right-curving cracks in the center of the face. **Pitch 1:** (5.6) The start is from near a huge pine

tree, directly below the twin cracks. There are two ways to start: Either paddle left on a slab, then walk back right on a ledge, or climb up more directly from a bit to the right. Either start leads to a short crack, then continue up a low-angle slab to a short groove leading to the "ski tracks." Climb the steep, bucketed face, following the left crack for the best pro (5.6) up to a big, loose block in the left crack. Avoid the block by traversing left to an undercling/reach up to a good ledge with a 2-bolt belay/rappel anchor (100 feet). **Pitch 2:** Climb a flake on the right, then traverse right to the main "left ski track" crack and follow this to where it ends at a small ledge with a fixed pin. Move up to another fixed pin that protects the classic "step-around": a no-hands balance move around the bulge to the right. Belay a few feet higher at a nice ledge (large stopper, 2- to 3-inch CDs). **Pitch 3:** Climb the left-facing corner/arête up to where it ends, then friction past a bolt on a slab (5.6) up to a horizontal crack/ledge. Follow this straight left, then climb above it up to a pine tree belay to finish. Some big cams (3 to 4 inches) are useful on the traverse. **Pro:** thin to 4 inches. **FA:** Chuck Wilts and Ray Van Aken, September 1947.

8. Left Ski Track, Direct Finish (5.8 PG) * On the third pitch, instead of traversing left at the top, climb straight up the headwall past a fixed pin to the top.

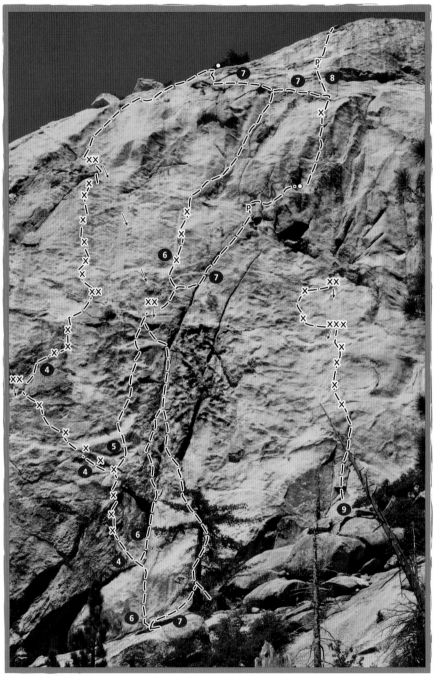

9. Chingadera (5.11a) **

Maybe the hardest face climb in America in 1967. Begin about 75 feet up and right from the "ski tracks." **Pitch 1:** Climb a crack (5.9) to reach a series of bolts. At the fourth bolt, move slightly left and up (5.11a) to a 3-bolt belay/rappel anchor (70 feet). **Pitch 2:** Traverse left (5.10+) to a bolt and up past another bolt (5.10b), then move right (5.10+) to a 2-bolt belay/rappel anchor (85 feet). Can be done as one pitch, but rope drag will be an issue. **Pro:** thin to 2 inches. **FA:** Bob Kamps and Mark Powell, February 1967.

Chingadera was named after a dog that Mark Powell had bet on in a dog race at Rapid City, South Dakota, shortly before the climb. The dog came in last place.

Bob Kamps led the first ascent of *Chingadera* in Cortina hiking boots, which were very stiff and allowed him to perform precise edging. According to 1960s climber Don Lauria, Kamps climbed in the Cortinas because he had very small, but wide feet (5 EEE), and they were the only high-quality boots available in his size.

Using his stiff Cortinas, along with his masterful edging technique, Kamps could stand and drill a bolt where others could barely let go to clip. Using these boots, Kamp made many first ascents and first free ascents of Tahquitz classics throughout the 1960s, and continued to climb hard up to the age of 74. Bob Kamps died of a sudden heart attack while on a route at a climbing gym in Los Angeles.

South Face—Right Side, Chingadera

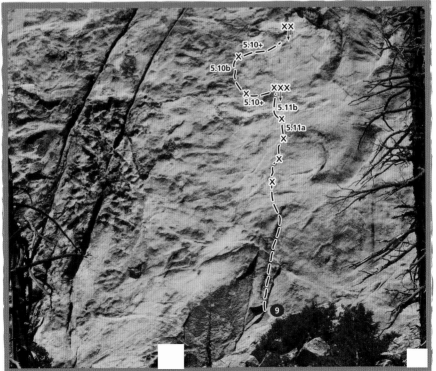

SOUTH FACE—RIGHT SIDE

This steep section of the wall is located about 100 yards to the right of The Open Book and about 200 feet to the right of the "ski tracks." It gets shade in the early morning, then is in the sun until very late in the day.

1. The Innominate (5.9 +) * This is the long, left-slanting crack system that forms an overhanging dihedral near the top. Begin about 100 feet right of *Chingadera*. **Pitch 1:** Climb up and left on a ramp (5.2), then climb about 20 feet up a steep crack (5.9) and belay. **Pitch 2:** Climb the right side of a pillar/block, then power up the crack in the slightly overhanging dihedral (5.9 +) to a nice ledge. **Pitch 3:** Climb up double cracks to finish on *Left Ski Track*, or follow a short flake on the right that blanks out, moving straight right on an unprotected (5.5 R) friction slab. Finish right on a big 3rd-class ramp to the top. **Pro:** to 3.5 inches. **FA:** (A2) Chuck Wilts and Gary Bloom, August 1947. **FFA:** Royal Robbins and Jerry Gallwas, 1957.

2. Pas de Deux (5.10c/d PG) ** Exciting face climbing up the bulging shield near the far right side of the great South Face. Start at a tree just right of the *Innominate* ramp. **Pitch 1:** Climb a scary mantle (5.10c/d, medium nut) up to a bolt. Move slightly left, then up (5.10b) to a small roof (small CD), then up and right on jugs (5.10a) to a slab where bolts protect sustained (5.10b/c) slab climbing.

South Face—Right Side

South Face—Far Right, Diddly

At the fifth bolt, climb up and left to a sixth bolt that protects a 5.10b move, or go up and slightly right past a bolt for an easier (5.9) finish. **Pitch 2:** A 4th-class ramp leads up and right to the top. **Pro:** medium nut, CDs from 0.3 to 2 inches. **FA:** Gib Lewis and Tobin Sorenson, May 1974.

3. Diddly (5.10a PG) * A sustained, slightly runout friction pitch up the ivory slab on the extreme far right side of the South Face. **Pitch 1:** Climb a right-facing flake (5.9) up to a fixed pin, over a small roof (5.9) to a bolt, up a little right-facing corner, then up the smooth slab past four more bolts, belaying at a small ledge at the base of a right-facing corner (2- to 3-inch gear). **Pitch 2:** (4th class) Up the corner, then head right on a ledge to the Friction Route Descent. **Pro:** to 3 inches. **FA:** Mark Powell and Bob Kamps, January 1967.

Suicide Rock Overview

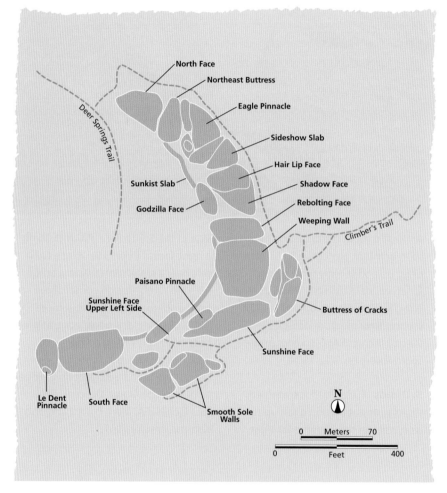

Deer Springs Trail

North Face

Northeast Buttress

Eagle Pinnacle

Sideshow Slab

Hair Lip Face

Sunkist Slab

Shadow Face

Godzilla Face

Rebolting Face

Weeping Wall

Climber's Trail

Paisano Pinnacle

Sunshine Face
Upper Left Side

Buttress of Cracks

Sunshine Face

Le Dent
Pinnacle

South Face

Smooth Sole
Walls

N

0	Meters	70
0	Feet	400

Suicide Rock

Getting there: From the town of Idyllwild, drive uphill (northeast) on either Pine Crest Avenue or North Circle Drive to where they intersect. Turn onto South Circle Drive and make an immediate left onto Fern Valley Road. From this turn, proceed 1.4 miles to Forest Drive and the Suicide Rock parking area (GPS: N33 45.980'/ W116 41.398'). Parking is along Forest Drive; a few spots are available along Fern Valley Road near the intersection with Forest Drive. (See Idyllwild Area map on page 6 and Tahquitz and Suicide Rocks Overview map on page vi and below.)

APPROACH TRAIL

The trail to Suicide Rock is less steep and strenuous than Tahquitz's Lunch Rock Trail, but still involves a climb of about 800 vertical feet in roughly 1.5 miles of hiking. The upper section (which is not maintained) is steep and rocky.

Suicide Rock Approach

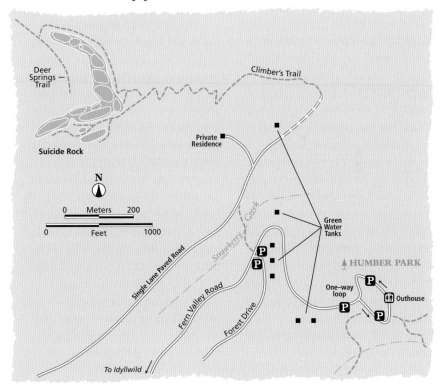

Suicide Rock Overview—Left Side

The trail begins from Fern Valley Road, just uphill from its intersection with Forest Drive, across from some huge green water tanks (GPS: N33 46.000' / W116 41.398'). (Humber Park is 0.2 mile farther up Fern Valley Road.) The trail begins by heading down some rustic stairs, then continues for about 100 feet, crosses a small stream (sometimes dry in late season), and after about another 100 feet intersects a paved, single-lane road. Turn right onto the paved road and follow it uphill until it turns into a dirt road, then fades into a trail. The trail cuts left, climbing gently along a slope until it reaches a sign that reads TRAIL NOT MAINTAINED BEYOND THIS POINT. From here it winds steeply up the hillside to Suicide Rock.

The first rock formation you'll see as you approach the base of the cliffs is the Buttress of Cracks. You'll come to a fork in the trail (GPS: N33 46.233' / W116 41.611'). The left fork will take you to the Buttress of Cracks at the base of the *Hernia* route. If you stay right, you'll come to another fork in the trail (GPS: N33 46.229' / W116 41.629'). Turn left and the trail continues a short distance to the Buttress of Cracks at the base of *Arcy Farcy*. Turn right and the trail zigzags up to the base of the Weeping Wall (stay left on this trail to avoid any subsidiary trails) (GPS: N33 46.219' / W116 41.658').

The routes are described from left to right (if you're facing the rock), and are divided into geographical areas, beginning with the South Face and

Suicide Rock Overview—Right Side

moving right to the Smooth Sole Walls, Sunshine Face, Buttress of Cracks, Weeping Wall, Rebolting Face, Shadow Face, Hair Lip Face, Sideshow Slab, Eagle Pinnacle, Northeast Buttress and North Face areas. Some of these areas have been further subdivided into sections. The approaches and descents are included in the introduction for each section of the rock.

Darrell Hensel
leading
*Someone
You're Not*
(5.13a) PHOTO
KEVIN POWELL

South Face

The South Face of Suicide Rock features panes of smooth, perfect granite with sheets of polished gold rock, quartz dikes, and a myriad of incut edges. Some of the very best face climbing that Suicide Rock has to offer is found here, along with the great slab testpiece of *Hades*. During the height of summer, the South Face is a very hot place, as it bakes in the sun until late in the day, only getting shade after about 4 p.m. The best time to climb here is during cooler weather.

Approach: The best approach to the South Face is made by following the trail left along the base of the Buttress of Cracks, scrambling up a 3rd-class gully to the base of the Sunshine Face, then up a gully to the top of the Smooth Sole Walls and through a notch with a distinctive, spade-shaped boulder. A boulder problem move here (about 5.8) is required to get to the top of the notch behind the Smooth Sole Walls. Traverse the top of the Smooth Sole Walls' left side to a point where you can scramble (short

South Face

section of 4th class) up to a rough trail that leads up and left to the expansive slab of the South Face. (See Suicide Rock—Left Side Overview map.)

An alternate approach is up through a short chimney near the base of the approach for the Sunshine Face's upper left side. This requires a bit of tunneling and chimney/stemming moves, and is about 5.6 in difficulty.

Descent: Several rappel descents are possible to get back to the base of the South Face, and are noted in the route descriptions and on the topos. To descend from the top of the cliff with one 60-meter rope, rappel 90 feet from bolts at the top of the face directly to the bolted rappel anchor on *Archangel.* From here you can rappel 80 feet to bolts on Twilight Ledge, then 50 feet to the ground.

LE DENT PINNACLE

This formation is left of the main South Face slab, and is guarded by a tough approach. It can be accessed by some difficult scrambling up and left from the base of the South Face. The easiest approach is actually from the top of Suicide Rock, descending a gully between Le Dent Pinnacle and Deception Pillar. This involves a bit of 5th-class downclimbing and tunneling under some chockstones, but is much easier than bushwhacking from the base of the South Face.

1. South Arête (5.11d) *** This route is a rarity for Suicide Rock—extremely steep face climbing. Climb a short crack to a spectacular arête/face with six bolts. **Descent:** Rappel 100 feet from slings on a horn. **Pro:** a few to 2 inches. The first ascent was a seriously bold ground-up lead done with only three bolts. **FA:** Tom Gilje and Scott Erler, January 1998.

DECEPTION PILLAR

This is the prominent 200-foot-high buttress bordering the left side of the main South Face cliff. **Approach:** From the far left side of the South Face's base, head up a ramp that diagonals up and left to the base of the crack/corner that separates Deception Pillar from the South Face slab. Make a move up a short crack to the right, then head up and right on ledges (4th class) to a big, flat ledge known as Twilight Ledge.

2. Brilliant Disguise (5.11a) ** From Twilight Ledge, move onto the pillar, traversing up and left past two bolts (5.11a), then climb a steep, knobby face (5.10a) past two more bolts on the outside face of the pillar. Runout but easy climbing takes you to the top. Belay at a pine tree (165 feet). **Descent:** From the top you can walk over to the bolts at the top of the South Face and rappel. **Pro:** to 3 inches. **FA:** Bob Gaines, Troy Mayr, Charles Cole, and Charlie Peterson, September 1987.

MAIN SOUTH FACE ROUTES

3. Hell's Angel (5.12a R) *** Start on the left side of the face, just right of a corner. Climb past overlaps to a scary (5.11b R) mantle to gain the third bolt, then go up and left past four bolts to a very thin slab crux at the top (5.12a) (2-bolt belay/rappel anchor). **Descent:** Rappel with two ropes to the ground, or rappel 80 feet to a ledge with a 2-bolt anchor, then 50 feet to the ground. **FA:** Bob Gaines, Paul Van Betten, and Jay Smith, June 1987.

4. Midnight Sun Variation (5.12a) ** From Twilight Ledge, climb straight up past bolts (moving right at the third bolt) to join *Hell's Angel* for its top section. **FA:** Bob Gaines, October 1999.

5. Archangel (5.11d) *** Start right of *Hell's Angel* (both routes share the fourth bolt), then go straight up past two more bolts to a 2-bolt anchor on a ledge. **Descent:** Rappel with two ropes to the ground, or rappel 80 feet to a ledge with a 2-bolt anchor, then 50 feet to the ground. **FA:** Darrell Hensel and Jonny Woodward, July 1986.

6. Hades (5.13a) *** Superb rock quality with a variety of fantastic moves and a super-thin and powerful crux on pitch 2. The first pitch is one of the great slab pitches of Idyllwild. Start 40 feet right of *Archangel* at the lowest point on the face. **Pitch 1:** Climb past bolts (5.9 R to the first bolt, then 5.10d to the second), then step right into a right-facing arch, up past two more bolts. Make crux moves where the arch curves right (5.12a), then climb over the arch up to a bolt that protects a thin face traverse left (5.11b) to easier climbing and a 2-bolt belay stance (150 feet). **Pitch 2:** Climb a thin, sharp flake, then up past a bolt (5.11c) and over a tiny roof to clip the second bolt, which protects the crux—a height-dependent, powerful, dynamic move off razor-thin sidepulls up and right to a good hold. From here it's a cruise to the top and a 2-bolt belay/rappel anchor. **Descent:** Rappel 80 feet back to the pitch 1 anchor, then rappel 150 feet to the ground. **FA:** (A3) Tobin Sorenson, et al., 1970s. **FFA pitch 1:** Kevin Powell and Darrell Hensel, 1980. **FFA pitch 2:** John Long and Bob Gaines, 1984.

7. Palm Sunday (5.11b) * Slap your way past a bolt up the short, sharp arête on the left side of the exfoliation slab. **Pro:** a small TCU. **FA:** Bob Gaines, Dwight Brooks, Paul Edwards, and John Long, June 1988.

8. Disco Jesus (5.11b) *** Another Suicide Rock slab classic, with great moves on great rock. **Pitch 1:** (5.10c) Jam the finger crack up the center of the exfoliation slab. **Pitch 2:** Climb tough moves (5.11b) just left of the belay, past an undercling, up to a bolt. The *Crucifixion* moves left from this point. Climb up and right past two bolts at a right-leaning corner, then

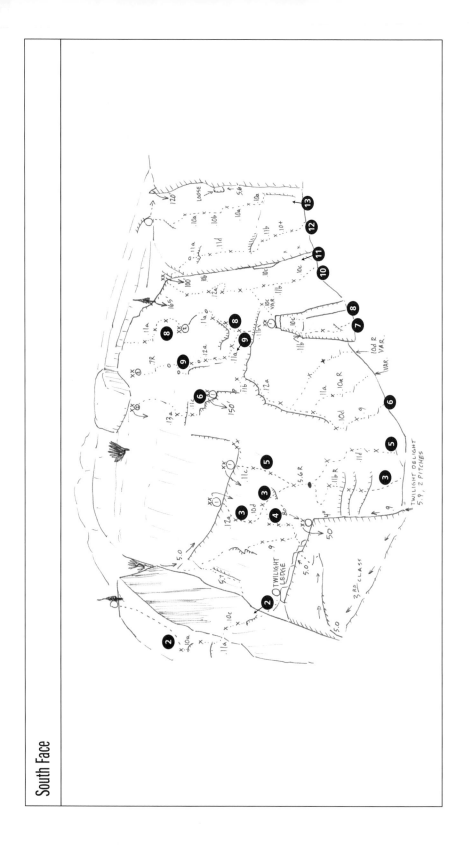

up to a dicey step-up to a knob. The 2-bolt belay is up and left from here. **Pitch 3:** Up the slab past three bolts to the top. Pitches 2 and 3 can be climbed in one 165-foot pitch, but you'll need to employ judicious use of long runners. **Pro:** thin to 2 inches. **FA:** Eric Erickson and others, 1978.

9. Crucifixion (5.12a) *** From the first bolt on the second pitch of *Disco Jesus,* tiptoe left across a quartz band past another bolt, then up a groove past three bolts to a very hard (5.12a) move to gain a knob. Continue past one more bolt (5.10b) to easier but highly runout (5.7 R) climbing up to a 2-bolt anchor. **FA:** Bob Gaines, August 1987.

10. Picante (5.12a) ** Begin 20 feet left of *Miscalculation*. Challenging 5.10c moves way off the deck get you to the first bolt, followed by 5.11b moves to the second bolt. At the fifth bolt, downclimb until you're level with the fourth bolt, move right about 10 feet, then follow a series of thin edges (5.12a) up to a scary move (5.11b) to gain the last bolt. From here, head up and right to *Miscalculation*. You can belay from *Miscalculation*'s bolt anchor at the top of the dihedral, but you'll protect your follower better if you head up higher and belay from a tree (165-foot rappel). **Pro:** to 2 inches. **FA:** John Long, Darrell Hensel, Kevin Powell, and Dave Wonderly, May 1987.

11. Miscalculation (5.10c) ** This is the smooth left-facing dihedral on the far right side of the face. Don't underestimate this one—it's harder than it looks, and the climbing is sustained with a variety of great moves. There are two bolts at the top (100-foot rappel). **Pro:** many thin to 3 inches, including CDs. **FA:** Ivan Couch and Mike Dent, 1970.

12. It's a Mayracole (5.11d) ** Troy Mayr and Charles Cole (founder of the 5.10 company and inventor of stealth and C4 rubber) teamed up for numerous Suicide Rock first ascents, and this is one of their many testpieces. Climb the continuously difficult, smooth slab just right of *Miscalculation* past five bolts, moving left at the top to the 2-bolt anchor (100 feet). The last bolt is a tough clip, and above that is a healthy (5.11a) runout. **Note:** There is an unfinished climb with two bolts just right of *Miscalculation,* this route is the next line of bolts to the right. **FA:** Troy Mayr and Charles Cole, July 1987.

13. 10b or no 10b (5.10b) * Climb about 40 feet up a huge right-facing corner (*Spring Cleaning,* 5.6), then move left and climb a very smooth friction slab past four bolts (gear anchor). **Descent:** Rappel 120 feet from slings on a horn at the top of *Spring Cleaning*. **Pro:** a few to 2.5 inches. **FA:** Troy Mayr and Charles Cole, July 1987.

Smooth Sole Walls

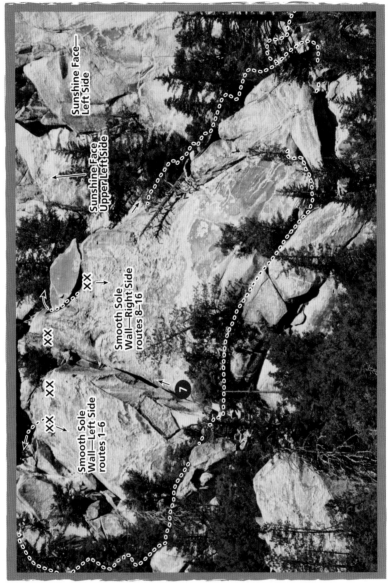

Sunshine Face—
Left Side

Sunshine Face—
Upper Left Side

Smooth Sole
Wall—Right Side
routes 8–16

Smooth Sole
Wall—Left Side
routes 1–6

7

Smooth Sole Walls

The Smooth Sole Walls are located several hundred feet to the left of and below the Sunshine Face, and consist of two separate, 100-foot-tall, high-angle slabs split by a deep chimney (*Chatsworth Chimney*). The climbing is characterized by smearing and crimping on edges, with the occasional huge knob thrown into the mix. The climbs are predominantly bolt protected and, in general, very runout. These cliffs face southeast and do not get shade until late afternoon during the summer season.

Approach: From where the trail to Suicide Rock meets the base of the cliff (at the right side of the Buttress of Cracks), scramble left (3rd class) and uphill along the base of the Buttress of Cracks cliffs for about 50 yards (passing the thin crack of *The Pirate*) to the base of the 300-foot-high Sunshine Face. Continue left until the trail steepens and begins to ascend a gully, then traverse left along a ledge around the corner. *Toxic Waltz* and *Tango* are directly above this point. To get to the Smooth Sole Wall's left side, continue under a wedged boulder and up and over another boulder, and you're at the base of *Pink Royd*. The remaining routes are found by scrambling about 100

feet up a slab (3rd class) to a flat area at the base of *Mickey Mantle*. (See Suicide Rock Overview on page 134.)

SMOOTH SOLE WALL— LEFT SIDE

Descent: Rappel from bolts (35 meters, 115 feet) at the top of the left side of the cliff, or downclimb (3rd class) to the far left.

1. Last Dance (5.10a R) * On the far left side of the face, climb a very thin crack (5.9) until it peters out, then up the face (5.10a R) to a 2-bolt anchor on top. **Pro:** many very thin to 0.75 inch. **FA:** Eric Erickson and Bill Squires, 1973.

2. Blown Out (5.10d) * Start 25 feet down and right from *Last Dance* and climb straight up the slab past four bolts to a 2-bolt anchor. **FA:** Greg Bender and Phil Warrender, May 1972.

3. Down and Out (5.10c) ** Climb a crack to a ledge, then up and left past six bolts to a 2-bolt anchor. **FA:** Gib Lewis and Jim Wilson, March 1974.

4. Drowned Out (5.10a R) ** Climb a crack to a ledge, then go right up the ledge/flake until a move to a pocket gets you to the first bolt, then up past two more bolts to a knob, moving right to finish up the arête. **FA:** J. Knutson and Phil Warrender, September 1972.

5. Over and Out (5.9 R) ** Same start as *Drowned Out,* but move farther right onto the top of the pedestal (2-bolt anchor here), then climb the arête past one bolt to the top. **FA:** Bob Gaines, Troy Mayr, and Mike Van Volkom, October 1987.

6. Steppin' Out (5.11d or 5.11a) ** Begin at the base of the pillar just left of *Chatsworth Chimney.* Climb past two bolts on the steep wall with unique pockets, then move left around the arête (5.11a) to the third bolt. Continue straight up (5.11d) or left and up (5.10d) to a 2-bolt anchor. Rappel from here, or continue up *Over and Out.* **FA:** Bob Gaines, October 1987.

Smooth Sole Wall–Left Side

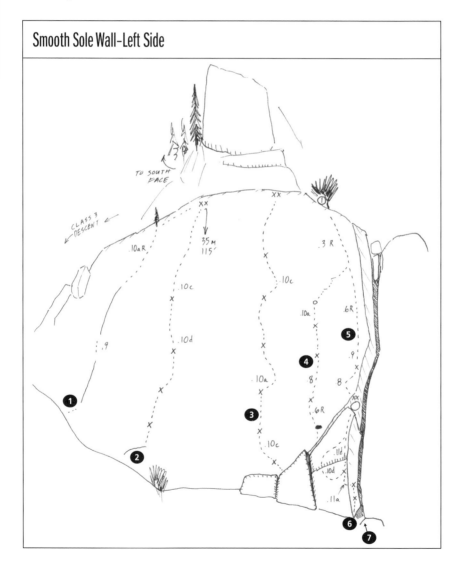

SMOOTH SOLE WALL— RIGHT SIDE

Descent: From the bolt anchor at the top of *Mickey Mantle,* you can rappel with one rope (100 feet) to the base. Beware the length, as the rope barely reaches the ground. You can also climb the ramp/chimney above the anchor (5.0) for about 40 feet to the top and scramble down and right, then back around to the base.

7. Chatsworth Chimney (5.8 R) * This is the deep chimney crack that divides the two Smooth Sole Walls, the left side of which forms a large corner. A lieback start gets you into a long pitch of chimney climbing with minimal pro. At the top of the chimney, move right up a crack (3-inch CD) to a 2-bolt anchor on top (165 feet). **Pro:** Small nut, 0.4- to 0.75-inch CDs, 3-inch CD. **FA:** Unknown.

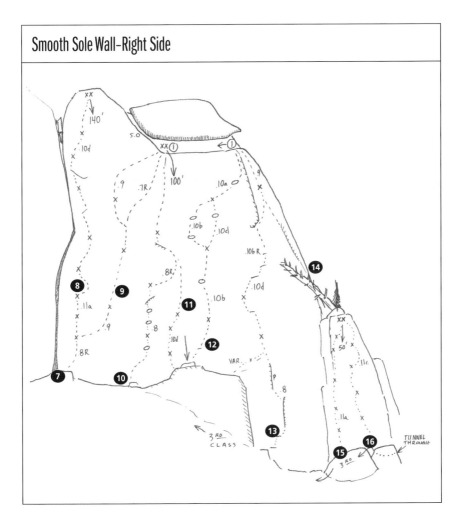

Smooth Sole Wall-Right Side

8. Battle of the Bulge (5.11a R) ** Begin just right of *Chatsworth Chimney*. Climb up to the first bolt of *The Fiend* (5.8 R), then straight up past seven more bolts to a 2-bolt anchor (140 feet). **FA:** Matt Cox, Randy Vogel, and Steve Emerson, 1976.

9. The Fiend (5.9 R) ** Begin just right of *Chatsworth Chimney,* with an unprotected slab (5.8 R) up to the first bolt. Traverse right and up (5.9) to the second bolt; after the third bolt, either go up and left past a fourth bolt (5.9) or up and right with no more bolts to the top (5.7 R, a safer route for the follower) and a 2-bolt anchor. **FA:** Jim Wilson and Phil Warrender, June 1972.

10. Mickey Mantle (5.8 R) *** Wonderful moves on great rock, with some long runouts that will keep you focused. Begin about 40 feet right of *Chatsworth Chimney.* Face climb and mantle a series of knobs past two bolts. At the second bolt, move right then up (5.8 R) to a sloping ledge, then move left to the final bolt that protects easier climbing to the top and a 2-bolt belay/rappel anchor. Rappel 100 feet or continue (5.0) up a short pitch to the top. **FA:** Jim Wilson and Phil Warrender, April 1972.

11. Howard's Fifty-Footer (5.10d R) Begin about 20 feet up and right from *Mickey Mantle* and climb the thin slab past three bolts to join *Mickey Mantle*

above its second bolt. 4 bolts to a 2-bolt anchor. **FA:** Paul Morrell and Scott Erler, June 1992.

12. Ultimatum (5.10b R) ** A unique mix of thin-hold slab climbing and large knobs. Start at the top of the pedestal 30 feet up and right from *Mickey Mantle.* There is a serious run-out above the first bolt getting up to a knob. At the second bolt, either climb out left, up, then back right to a large knob (5.10b) and a third bolt, or climb straight up to the knob and the third bolt (5.10d). From the third bolt, move up and right to another humongous knob, then up to a ledge at the top. **Pro:** slings for large knobs, gear anchor, 1.5-to 3-inch CDs. **Descent:** Rappel from the *Mickey Mantle* anchor (100 feet). **FA:** John Long and Gib Lewis, April 1972.

13. Pink Royd (5.10d R) * Begin about 50 feet down and right from *Ultimatum,* to the right of a right-facing corner, at the base of the lower right side of the cliff. Climb loose flakes (5.8) to a fixed pin, then up the slab past two bolts, with a thin edge crux (5.10d) right above the second bolt, then run it out (5.10- R) up to a flake (2-inch CD). Move right to join *Sensuous Corner* at its bolt. **Descent:** Rappel from the *Mickey Mantle* bolt anchor (100 feet). **Pro:** 1.5- to 3-inch CDs, gear anchor. **FA:** Eric Erickson and John Long, 1972.

Kelly Karrigan leads *Mickey Mantle* (5.8)
PHOTO GREG EPPERSON

14. Sensuous Corner (5.9) * Begin halfway up the right edge of the Smooth Sole Wall's right side. Climb a crack leading to a narrow prow where a bolt protects unusual moves up to the top. **Pro:** CDs from 0.75 to 3 inches. **FA:** Gib Lewis and G. Labadie, 1973.

15. Tango (5.11a) * This climb is the left of two routes directly above the boulder you tunnel under on the approach, at the far lower right section of the cliff on a small, separate buttress. Crimp, smear, and edge past five bolts to a 2-bolt belay/rappel anchor (50 feet). The crux is getting to the second bolt. **FA:** Bob Gaines and Frank Bentwood, June 2010.

16. Toxic Waltz (5.11c) * This climb is the right of two short routes located directly above the boulder you tunnel under on the approach. Hard smearing and edging lead past four bolts to a 2-bolt belay/rappel anchor (50 feet). **FA:** Geoff Archer, Kay Buskirk, and Terry McCarthy, July 1989.

11

Sunshine Face

This magnificent cliff is the largest face at Suicide Rock, home of the ultra-classic *Sundance* (5.10b) and the legendary *Valhalla* (5.11b). The rock quality is impeccable, and the face climbs can only be described as superb.

It faces southeast and is in the sun until late afternoon. In the summer it doesn't get shade until almost 3 p.m. Paisano Pinnacle is the large block that sits on top of the face, jutting out slightly to form a roof. *Paisano Overhang* is the roof crack that splits the ceiling formed by the protruding block. The Sunshine Face is framed on the left by *Paisano Chimney* and on the right by *Buttress Chimney*.

Approach: From the point where the trail up to Suicide Rock meets the base of the cliff (at the right side of the Buttress of Cracks), head left along the base of Buttress of Cracks; a short 3rd-class scramble leads up to a level spot at the base of *The Pirate*. *Insomnia Crack* is just around the corner to the right, as is the impressive Sunshine Face.

SUNSHINE FACE—
UPPER LEFT SIDE

This is the face to the left of Paisano Pinnacle, separated by a deep cleft (*Paisano Chimney*).

Approach: Walk along the base of the main Sunshine Face, then up the loose rock- and tree-filled gully. A bit of scrambling (4th class) up slabs and ledges gets you to the base of the cliff.

Descent: Rappel with two ropes (165 feet) from bolts at the top of *Chisholm Trail,* or walk down and right to the rappel anchors on a slab across from the top of Paisano Pinnacle. Rappel 80 feet to a large ledge (the top of the main Sunshine Face), then rappel 100 feet from bolts on the far right (east) side of the ledge to 4th-class downclimbing that takes you to the base of the Weeping Wall.

1. Chisholm Trail (5.11c) ** This route climbs a crack in a right-facing flare on the face between two long chimney systems on the left side of the cliff. Face climb (5.10a) up to the crack, then jam a difficult section (5.11c) up to a bolt. Easier crack climbing (5.10c) leads to a 2-bolt belay/rappel anchor (165 feet). **Pro:** thin to 3 inches. **FA:** Fred Ziel, Eric Erickson, and Tim Powell, 1977.

2. The Man Who Fell to Earth

(5.11a) ** This is the golden face just right of a deep chimney (called *B.C.'s Ouch Chimney*, 5.9). Climb shallow, discontinuous thin cracks, then up a gold slab. 7 bolts to a gear anchor. **Descent:** Climb to the top, then down and around to the left, downclimbing (4th class) to the bolt anchor for *Chisholm Trail,* and rappel 165 feet. **Pro:** thin to 2-inch CDs. **FA:** Fred Ziel and Tim Powell, 1978.

3. Caliente (5.12c) ** A monument

to the talent of John Bachar, this was one of America's toughest face routes in the 1970s, and still tests many aspiring climbers today. Begin about 40 feet left of *Paisano Chimney.* Scramble up and right to a ledge/ramp to a ledge with a 2-bolt anchor.

A 5.11d direct start can also be done on the slab below and right (6 bolts, **FA:** John Weinberg, 2012). Climb a left-facing flake, then face climb up to a bolt. Good 5.10 climbing leads past two more bolts to a steep headwall with doubled bolts that protect the crux: thin, reachy, and powerful crimping on small edges. After the crux a 5.10d move gets you up to a left-curving arch with a 2-bolt anchor partway up it (optional belay here). Continue up the arch (5.10c R), or move right and climb the face and crack just above the arch (5.10d R). **Descent:** Climb up to the top, then down and around to the left, downclimbing (4th class) to the bolt anchor for *Chisholm Trail,* and rappel 165 feet. **Pro:** thin to 2 inches. **FA:** John Bachar, 1978.

Sunshine Face—Upper Left Side

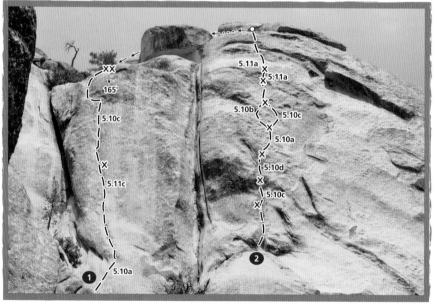

4. Someone You're Not (5.13a) ***
It took slab master Darrell Hensel
numerous on-sight attempts before
deciphering the miraculous crux,
which is both delicate yet powerful.
The route has only been repeated

once in twenty years. **Pitch 1:** Start
up *Paisano Chimney,* and belay at
bolts atop the *Clockwork Orange* pillar.
Pitch 2: Climb a slightly runout slab
(5.10c) past three bolts to a steeper
headwall of darker rock (*Caliente*

Sunshine Face—Upper Left Side

climbs through the left side of this same headwall). Steep edging past two more bolts on the headwall gets you to the sixth bolt and the baffling (5.13a) crux. Above this it's a cruise (5.10d) past three more bolts to the top and a gear anchor (1- to 3-inch CDs). **Pro:** pro to 3 inches. **FA:** Darrell Hensel, November 1991.

5. Paisano Chimney (5.8) This is the long chimney that marks the right boundary of the Sunshine Face's upper left side. It forms the gap between Paisano Pinnacle and the main cliff. **Pro:** to 4 inches. **FA:** Pat Callis and Lee Harrell, May 1968.

6. Clockwork Orange (5.10d) * Begin at the start of *Paisano Chimney*. Climb a crack to a tricky arête with three bolts, ending on a flat ledge atop a block-like pinnacle with a 2-bolt anchor (100-foot rappel). **Pro:** to 1.5 inches. **FA:** Kelly Vaught, Bob Gaines, and Frank Bentwood, July 1998.

Sunshine Face—Upper Left Side

MAIN SUNSHINE FACE

The following routes are located on the main sector of the Sunshine Face, to the right of *Paisano Chimney* and to the left of *Buttress Chimney*. All the routes end at the large ledge to the right of Paisano Pinnacle called Paisano Ledge.

Descent: Look for bolts at the far (east) end of the Paisano Ledge (hidden from view by a boulder). Three

rappels: 100 feet, 100 feet, then 80 feet (to the *Sundance* anchors) from here reach the ground.

With two ropes you can rappel 165 feet to the *Hesitation/New Generation* anchor, then 165 feet to the ground.

You can also rappel from bolts at the top of the *Bye Gully*. These bolts are located at the far right (east) end of the ledge. Rappel 100 feet plus

Main Sunshine Face–Left Side

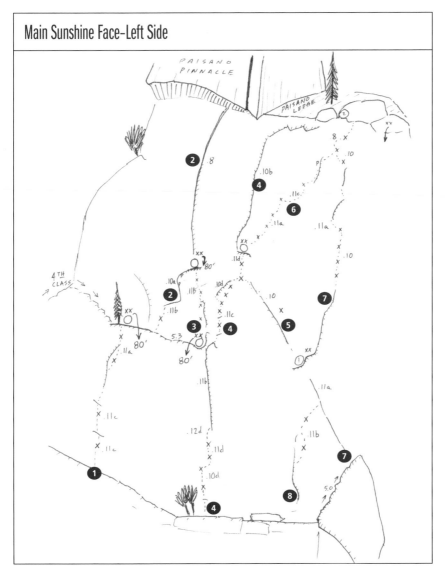

Main Sunshine Face/Weeping Wall Rappels

4th class

Paisano Pinnacle

Sunshine Face— Upper Left Side

XX

80'

XX XX

Weeping Wall

XX

165'

100'

Main Sunshine Face

class 4'

165'

XX

100'

XX

XX

80'

165'

Buttress of Cracks

some 4th-class downclimbing (or 165 feet and some 3rd-class downclimbing) to the base of the Weeping Wall, and from here hike down the trail, around the base of the Buttress of Cracks, and back up to the base of the Sunshine Face.

1. Gates of Delirium (5.11c) * Only the first pitch is described here, as the second pitch is somewhat of a mystery. Thin crimps past two bolts (5.11c) lead to a corner with two bolts (5.11a), ending at a ledge with a 2-bolt belay/rappel anchor just right of a pine tree. **Descent:** Rappel 80 feet or downclimb (4th class) off to the left. **Pro:** thin to 2 inches. **FA:** Tony Yaniro and Richard Leversee, January 1976.

2. The Drain Pipe (5.11b) ** Start from the bolt anchor on the ledge at the top of the first pitch of *Gates of Delirium*. This can be accessed by 4th-class climbing in from the far left side of the ledge. **Pitch 1:** Crank thin moves past a bolt (5.11b) to gain an S-shaped crack with fixed pins (5.10a) that leads to a small belay ledge. **Pitch 2:** (5.8) Jam up the "drain pipe," a spectacular 3- to 6-inch-wide crack that leads to the Paisano Pinnacle ceiling, then hand traverse right to Paisano Ledge. **Pro:** to 4.5 inches. **FA:** (5.7, A1) Lee Harrell and Charlie Raymond, March 1967. **FFA:** John Long, Richard Harrison, and Rick Accomazzo, 1973.

3. Last of the Mohicans (5.11b) ** **Pitch 1:** Start at the bolt anchor on the ledge at the top of the first pitch of *Gates of Delirium*. Access by climbing in (4th class) from the far left side of the ledge. Continue walking right on the ledge until it peters out, then hand traverse right on a flake for about 40 feet (exposed 5.3) to a 2-bolt belay anchor. **Pitch 2:** Climb straight up the slab past four bolts on incredible bronze patina up to the 2-bolt belay/rappel anchor for *The Drain Pipe*. Continue up *The Drain Pipe*, or descend in two short (80-foot) rappels or one long (35-meter, 115-foot) rappel to the ground. **Pro:** to 4.5 inches for *The Drain Pipe* finish. **FA:** Bob Gaines, Frank Bentwood, Chip Maloney, July 2001.

4. Ishi (5.12d) *** A long pitch of 5.10 to 5.11 climbing, punctuated by one of the area's thinnest cruxes. Start about 50 feet right of *Gates of Delirium*, behind a large oak tree.

According to Darrell Hensel, who did the landmark first free ascent of *Ishi* in 1985, "Ishi was the last native American Indian known to be living in the wild around the turn of the century. The route was not renamed when it was done free since the existing name seemed so fitting; *Ishi* was the last aid route to be freed on the Sunshine Face and at Suicide."

Pitch 1: Crimp past a 4-bolt ladder (5.11d) to the crux—a long reach up to a narrow, 40-foot long, left-facing corner (5.12d). Lieback the corner (5.11b, protection is difficult without preplaced protection or fixed pitons) up to a small ledge and possible belay at two bolts on the left. (First free ascensionist Darrell Hensel eschewed belaying at the ledge, preferring one long pitch.) Continue up and right on ledges to the start of the upper 7-bolt ladder. Crank up edges past three bolts (5.11c), moving left at the third bolt (skipping the fourth bolt) and up a small flake (5.10d), then moving right from the top of the flake to the sixth bolt of the ladder and cranking a very thin edging move (5.11d) above the seventh bolt up to a 2-bolt anchor. The seventh bolt is shared with *Quiet Desperation*. **Pitch 2:** (5.10b) Lieback a classic thin flake, similar to Yosemite's *Wheat Thin*. If this exhilarating pitch were more accessible, it would be very popular. You *can* access this superb pitch another way: Build a gear anchor at Paisano Ledge, rappel down to the *Ishi* bolt anchor (100 feet), then climb back out. **Pro:** to 2.5 inches. **FA:** (A3) Tony Zeek, et al. **FA, upper bolt ladder** (5.11c): Gib Lewis, Rick Accomazzo, and Jim Wilson, March 1976. **FFA, entire route:** Darrell Hensel, 1985.

5. Quiet Desperation (5.11d) **
Pitch 1: Climb the first pitch of *Iron Cross*. **Pitch 2:** Climb diagonally up and left past a bolt on a razor-thin flake, then up a short and desperate face (5.11d) past two bolts to the 2-bolt anchor shared with *Ishi*. **Pitch 3:** Lieback the spectacular thin flake (5.10b) up to Paisano Ledge. **Pro:** thin to 2.5 inches. **FA:** Rick Accomazzo, Gib Lewis, and Jim Wilson, March 1976.

6. Golden Oldies (5.11c) ** This variation climbs a beautiful gold slab, beginning at the *Ishi/Quiet Desperation* bolt anchor. From the anchor, move right and up past four bolts (5.11a), traversing right (5.11c) from the fourth bolt to a rest stance. Climb a 5.10a move to the fifth bolt, then follow a thin left-facing corner (5.9) with a fixed pin (you can back up the pin with a small nut). Step right and join *Iron Cross* for its last two bolts (5.8). Belay from a pine tree at Paisano Ledge. **Pro:** one small nut. **FA:** Bob Gaines, Kelly Vaught, Frank Bentwood, and Chip Maloney, July 2001.

7. Iron Cross (5.11a PG) *** A fantastic route on fabulous rock. Start by traversing right from the base of *Ishi* across a ledge to a massive, arrowhead-shaped flake. **Pitch 1:** Climb to the top of the flake, then follow the left-leaning, hard to protect (thin nuts, TCUs) thin crack (5.11a PG) to a nice ledge with a 2-bolt anchor. **Pitch 2:** Up a left-facing corner to a beautiful face with four bolts and the crux—the infamous "iron cross" move that unlocks the sequence up to a corner with fixed pins. Above this, wind past three more bolts to the top. Belay from a pine tree on Paisano Ledge. **Pro:** many thin to 1.5 inches. **FA:** (5.10, A2) Charlie Raymond and Pat Callis, May 1968. **FFA pitch 1:** Gib Lewis and Tobin Sorenson, 1973. **FFA complete route:** John Long and Richard Harrison, July 1973.

8. Red Rain (5.11b PG) ** This quality variation begins just left of the massive flake. Climb a thin corner up to a face with two bolts, then move right to join the crux of the first pitch of *Iron Cross*. **Pro:** thin nuts and TCUs/ CDs. **FA:** Dave Evans and Darrell Hensel, August 1986.

MAIN SUNSHINE FACE—RIGHT SIDE

9. Moondance (5.11c) *** Sustained thin-hold face and slab climbing up a pane of gorgeous golden rock. **Pitch 1:** Climb *Sundance* up to the base of the lieback and set up a belay (big cams). **Pitch 2:** Move left to where the face steepens (thin cams to 0.75 inch), crank up past two bolts (5.11c), then angle up and right on the slab past six more bolts (a long sling on the right-most bolt helps reduce rope drag) to a delicate, nerve-racking runout (5.9 R) up to a 3-bolt belay/rappel anchor. You can rappel from here to the *Sundance* Log Ledge anchor with two ropes or a 70-meter rope (35 meters, 115 feet). **Pitch 3:** Climb 5.10 moves directly above the belay to a

set of two bolts, then move up and right, clipping the last two bolts of the *Sundike* finish to the top. You can avoid the lower 5.11c crux by traversing left from the *Sundance* bolt belay on Log Ledge to the third bolt for an easier (5.11a) but still classic variation. **FA:** (from Log Ledge) Dave Evans and Craig Fry, June 1986. **FA direct start:** Darrell Hensel and Dave Evans, September 1986.

10. Sundance (5.10b) *** My pick for the best 5.10 face climb in Idyllwild. **Pitch 1:** Begin in a short dihedral. Stem and jam up the corner (5.9), then hand traverse right on a horizontal crack, then up a slab to a big left-facing corner and a short but very steep, strenuous lieback (5.9, 4-inch CD) up to a 2-bolt belay/rappel anchor at Log Ledge (the log is long gone). **Pitch 2:** Crank a steep, thin face move off Log Ledge to a flake/ledge with a bolt, then climb the knobby face past four more bolts, making a delicate traverse right from the fourth bolt over to a corner. Follow the arête just right of the corner (5.6 R) up to a 3-bolt belay/rappel anchor (100-foot rappel to Log Ledge, 165 feet to the ground). **Pitch 3:** Climb straight up past two bolts to a tricky, hard to protect thin crack (or do the safer and more popular *Sundike* finish) that leads to the top. A 1-inch CD is useful at the top so you can traverse right and belay from the bolted rappel station. **Pro:** a few thin

Chris Miller and Cheryl Basye on the second pitch of *Sundance* (5.10b)

PHOTO KEVIN POWELL

nuts and CDs to 1 inch, plus a big (3- to 4.5-inch) cam or two. **FA:** Pat Callis, Charlie Raymond, and Larry Reynolds, January 1967.

11. Sundike (5.10a) *** This more popular and better-protected finish to *Sundance* veers left from the second bolt on the last pitch, climbing up and left on a white dike past two more bolts. **FA:** Clark Jacobs and Bob Harvey, March 1984.

12. Valhalla (5.11a) *** In the 1970s the only prerequisite to join the ranks of the elite and infamous club known as the "Stonemasters" was to climb this route. Start on a big ledge near the center of the Sunshine Face, just right of a tree. **Pitch 1:** A 5.9 mantle gets you to the first bolt, then slippery smearing (5.11a) up to a second bolt. Move right, up a ramp, and to a third bolt, then traverse up and left to a 2-bolt anchor on the lower right side of Log ledge (the log is long gone). **Pitch 2:** Traverse right on a ledge to a bolt, crank past the thin crux (5.11a), then wind your way past six more bolts up to a hanging 2-bolt belay (80-foot rappel to Log ledge). **Pitch 3:** Run it out (5.10a) up to a bolt, climb up and left to the first bolt on the third pitch of *Sundance,* then climb up and right past one more bolt to a crack in a corner that leads to the top. **Pro:** 0.75- to 1.5-inch CDs. **FA:** Ivan Couch, Larry Reynolds, and Mike Dent, November 1970.

13. Nirvana (5.11a) *** Begin just right of *Valhalla* and climb a series of scoops up a smooth slab past four bolts, then move left on ledges and climb directly up to the crux of *Valhalla*'s second pitch, clipping seven more bolts. **FA:** Bob Gaines and John Long, August 1986.

14. New Generation (5.11c) *** A new, younger generation of climbers (Mike Graham and Tobin Sorenson, ages 17 and 18 years old, respectively) flabbergasted the old guard and raised the standards with this classic testpiece in July 1973. **Pitch 1:** Begin on the lowest right part of the face, right of a left-facing corner. Climb a thin seam (5.9) up to a first bolt that protects a tricky move on slippery rock (5.11a), then up to a second bolt. Traverse left (5.10b) to the third bolt, from where you can either climb straight up (5.10c) or farther left then up (5.10c) to a 2-bolt anchor on No Go Ledge (70 feet). **Pitch 2:** A dicey (5.10d), unprotected move gets you to the first bolt, then crimp through the crux (5.11c) to the second bolt. Easier (5.10c) climbing gets you to a third bolt where the climbing eases (5.8) up to a small ledge with a 3-bolt belay/rappel anchor shared with *Hesitation* (165-foot rappel to the ground, 100 feet to No Go Ledge). **Pitch 3:** (5.10b) Climb the face to the right past four bolts to a crack that leads to the top. **Pro:** 0.75- to 1.5-inch CDs.

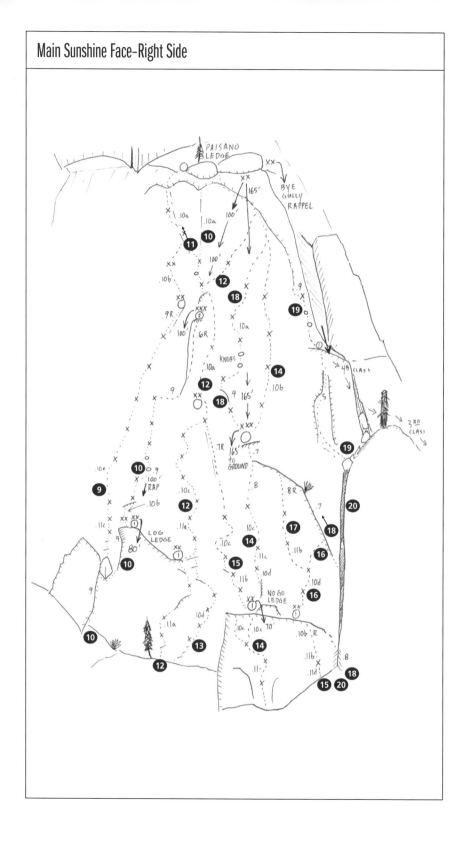

15. Race with the Devil (5.11d R) **
Pitch 1: Begin 30 feet right of *New Generation,* where a lone bolt marks the first pitch. Extremely thin face climbing (5.11d) gets you to the bolt, then it's a serious runout (5.10b R) with groundfall potential up to No Go Ledge and a 2-bolt belay anchor. **Pitch 2:** Shift the belay to the set of bolts farther left and climb the slab left of *New Generation,* up and left past four bolts (5.11b) to unprotected (5.7 R) face climbing up a dike to the join the second pitch of *Valhalla* at its last bolt. Above the fourth bolt you can also climb up and right (5.8 R) to the *Hesitation* belay. **Pro:** thin to 2 inches. **FA:** Tony Yaniro, 1979.

16. Hesitation Direct (5.10d) ** From the two-bolt belay at the right end of No Go Ledge, climb past two bolts (5.10d), then traverse up and right to join *Hesitation.* **Pro:** thin to 2 inches. **FA:** John Long, Jim Wood, and Clark Jacobs, 1975.

17. Voodoo Child Variation (5.11b) ** After clipping the second bolt on *Hesitation Direct,* traverse up and left (5.11b) to a third bolt, up easier climbing to a fourth bolt, then run it out (5.8) up to the ledge/ramp on *Hesitation.* **Pro:** thin to 2 inches. **FA:** John Long and Eric Erickson, 1978.

18. Hesitation (5.10a) ** **Pitch 1:** Climb about 80 feet up *Buttress Chimney* (stemming up the flare at the

bottom is tricky 5.8), then move left up a ramp/flake, finishing with a few face moves up to a bolted belay. **Pitch 2:** Meander up and left, then back up and right, passing five bolts and big knobs you can tie off for pro. **Pro:** small to 3 inches. **FA:** Pat Callis (rope solo!), July 1967.

19. The Stretch (5.9) * Although technically on the Sunshine Face, this route is best approached from the base of the Weeping Wall. Begin up and left from the Weeping Wall, at the notch at the top of the Buttress of Cracks. **Pitch 1:** Downclimb a few feet, then climb a juggy (5.5) crack system for about 80 feet to a ledge on the right. **Pitch 2:** Climb up knobs on the airy crest to a bolt, then move left (5.9) to a crack that is followed up to Paisano Ledge. Most parties climb just the second pitch, accessed by climbing about 60 feet up the *Bye Gully* (4th class) and belaying from the same ledge. **Pro:** to 3 inches. **FA:** Pat Callis and Charlie and Trish Raymond, November 1966.

20. Buttress Chimney (5.8) This is the deep chimney that borders the right side of the main Sunshine Face, listed here since it's used as an approach to access No Go Ledge and *Hesitation.* The crux is stemming the flared corner at the bottom, which is rather unprotected. **Pro:** to 3 inches. **FA:** Pat Callis and Lee Harrell, 1967.

Buttress of Cracks Overview

12.

Buttress of Cracks

The Buttress of Cracks is the lowest cliff band on Suicide Rock, and is the first section of rock you encounter on the approach trail, near the cliff's far right side. From where the approach trail meets the base of the rock, head left along the base of the Buttress of Cracks; a short uphill scramble (3rd class) leads to a small, flat spot near the left end of the Buttress (*The Pirate,* a very thin, straight crack, is located here). *Insomnia* and the immense Sunshine Face are just a short distance farther along the trail (see Suicide Rock Overview map).

Descent: For routes that top out on the Buttress of Cracks, scramble up and through a slot (4th class), then down to the notch behind the Buttress of Cracks. Head right, downclimbing (3rd class) to the base of the Weeping Wall, then follow the trail back down around to the base of the Buttress of Cracks. Rappel descents from the various routes are noted in the route descriptions.

1. Insomnia (5.11b/c) *** This stellar crack climb splits a slightly overhanging wall at the far left end of the Buttress of Cracks,

around the corner just left of *The Pirate,* facing the Sunshine Face. Begin by stemming up the flared corner of *Buttress Chimney* (5.8) to a small ledge about 25 feet up. Many climbers opt to set up a belay here. Climb a flared chimney (5.9), then jam or lieback the crack leading out of the chimney (crux) up to a thin hand crack that

Buttress of Cracks—Left Side

slants left (5.10d, harder if you have big hands) up to a 3-bolt anchor on top (35 meters, 115 feet). **Descent:** With a 60-meter rope you can rappel down (barely), plus a little down-climbing. **Pro:** to 3 inches. **FA:** (A3) Pat Callis and Larry Reynolds, June 1967. **FFA:** Jim Erickson and Scott Stewart, March 1972.

2. Double Exposure (5.10c, A1) **
This route climbs the spectacular arête formed by the left edge of the Buttress of Cracks. The start is just right of *Buttress Chimney* and left of and around the corner from *The Pirate*. Although some shenanigans are required to get started, once on the arête the face climbing is superb. A shoulder stand and two aid bolts

gain the arête, where four bolts are found for protection (5.10c). At the third bolt on the arête (fifth bolt on the climb), move up and right to a crack, then back left to the arête and up to a bolt anchor on top. A direct start (5.12b R) can be done past two widely spaced bolts on the lower right side of the arête. **Pro:** to 1 inch. **FA:** John Long, et al., 1975.

3. The Pirate (5.12c/d or 5.9, C2) ***
This aesthetic thin crack splits the blank wall at the far left end of the Buttress of Cracks. **Pitch 1:** Most often climbed as a practice aid route (A2 or C2) since it can be aided clean with nuts and small cams, with a short pendulum at the top to swing right to the belay. As a free climb this is a stout

Buttress of Cracks—Left Side

Lynn Hill leading *The Pirate* (5.12c/d), 1993 Photo Greg Epperson

4. Pieces of Eight (5.10d R) * No topo. From the bolt anchor on the first pitch of *The Pirate,* go straight up a dike past three bolts, joining the crack on *The Pirate* at the very top (2-bolt belay/rappel anchor, 100 feet). **Pro:** to 3 inches. **FA:** Bob Gaines and Mike Van Volkom, June 1987.

5. Captain Hook (5.8) * This is the obvious, deep chimney 25 feet right of *The Pirate.* Some delicate (5.8) face climbing gets you into the crack leading to the chimney, the crux of which is negotiating the "crocodile's head," a large chockstone near the top (5.7). **Pitch 2:** (5.7) Climb a crack to another chimney (dubbed "the throat") up to the top. **Pro:** to 3 inches. **FA:** Charlie Raymond and Larry Reynolds, October 1966.

6. Buccaneer (5.10c) This route is commonly done to set up a toprope on the first pitch of *The Pirate* and is also a good approach pitch for *Pieces of Eight.* From near the top of the first pitch of *Captain Hook,* climb up and left to where a bolt protects face climbing (5.10c) up to *The Pirate*'s bolt anchor (80 feet). **Pro:** to 3 inches. **FA:** Unknown.

lead (5.12+) up to a 2-bolt belay/rappel anchor (80 feet). **Pitch 2:** Climb up and left (5.9) to a 5.8 crack that leads to the top and a 2-bolt belay/rappel anchor (100 feet). **Pro:** many very thin nuts and CDs to 3 inches. **FA:** (5.8, A2) Pat Callis and Larry Reynolds, June 1967. **FFA:** Tony Yaniro, 1978.

Buttress of Cracks—Left Side

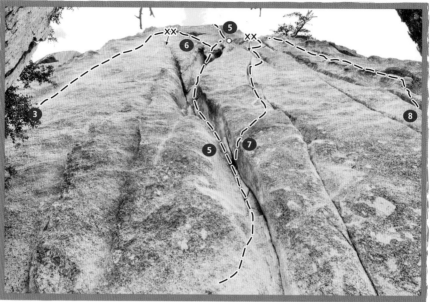

7. Pass Time (5.9) Start by climbing about 15 feet up *Captain Hook,* then move right to the first crack system just right of *Captain Hook* to a ledge with a shared 2-bolt belay/rappel anchor (100 feet if you swing left at the bottom). **Pro:** thin to 2 inches. **FA:** Phil Gleason and Lee Harrell, March 1968.

8. Frustration (5.10a) * Begin about 25 feet downhill from *Captain Hook* and climb twin vertical cracks (5.10a) up into a wide crack that leads up to a ledge with a shared 2-bolt belay/rappel anchor (100 feet if you swing left at the bottom). **Pro:** thin to 3 inches. **FA:** Pat Callis and Lee Harrell, March 1968.

Buttress of Cracks—Hernia

9. Hernia (5.8) * Start just left of the lowest point on the Buttress of Cracks. Climb a flake system (a bit loose) up to a small overlap, most easily passed by stepping right, then back left into a groove. Follow the crack as it curves up and right to a sloping ledge with a 2-bolt belay/rappel anchor (100 feet). **Pro:** thin to 3 inches. **FA:** Lee Harrell and S. Wood, August 1967.

10. Hernia Direct Finish (5.10a) * A popular finish that really adds to the pitch. Just before where the regular route traverses right to the bolt anchor, step up and left to a bolt that protects face climbing (5.10a) up to a flake that leads to a big ledge with a huge pine tree. Rappel from the tree (80 feet) over to the gully on the right. (165-foot pitch). **FA:** Ivan Couch and Mike Dent, 1969.

Buttress of Cracks—Right Side

11. Bacon Bits (5.11b/c R) * Scary to lead due to stout moves with a bad landing to reach the first bolt, but easily toproped from the 2-bolt anchor. Begin just right of *Hernia*. Crank some height-dependent moves (5.10+) to reach a bolt, then climb a flake system up to a face with four bolts heading up and right to a 2-bolt belay/rappel anchor (100-foot rappel). **Pro:** 0.5 to 1.5 inches. **FA:** Russ Clune, October 1987. **First lead:** Kelly Vaught, Clark Jacobs, and Rick Harlin, November 2000.

12. Winter Solstice (5.11c PG) ** The quintessential Suicide Rock slab pitch—thin, crimpy, sustained, and run-out. A bold lead but easily toproped off the *Hernia*'s 2-bolt anchor. Begin just right of *Bacon Bits*. Climb a thin flake up to a bolt, then crank thin (5.10d) moves up to ledges, then friction and crimp up the slab past four bolts to the top and a 2-bolt belay/rappel anchor (100 feet). **FA:** Hamilton Collins and Greg Rzonka, December 21, 1985.

13. Arcy Farcy (5.11a PG/R) * This runout, 3-bolt friction slab climb just left of a gully goes up to a ledge with a 2-bolt belay/rappel anchor (100 feet). It's getting harder over the years as tiny flakes disappear. The crux is at the first bolt; climb past it slightly to the right. Above, the climbing gets progressively easier—5.10b above the second bolt, 5.10a above the third bolt (100-foot rappel). **FA:** Mike Kaeser, Greg Bender, Phil Warrender, and Jim Wilson, 1972.

BUTTRESS OF CRACKS— UPPER RIGHT SIDE

These climbs are located on the upper right end of the Buttress of Cracks, which faces the base of the Weeping Wall. Where the trail up to Suicide Rock first gains sight of the rock, you'll come to a fork in the trail. Take the right fork, which winds uphill about 200 feet to the base of the Weeping Wall. The climbs on the Buttress of Cracks are immediately to your left.

Descent: Climb up to and through a notch (4th class) at the top of the Buttress, then head right (3rd class) back down around to the base of the Weeping Wall.

1. Low Pressure (5.10c) * A steep, strenuous lieback (5.10c) up a flared crack in a right-facing dihedral leads to a roof. Undercling out right, turn the roof (5.10a), then climb flakes to the top. **Pro:** 0.5- to 3-inch CDs. **FA:** Tobin Sorenson and Gib Lewis, 1973.

2. Warm Up (5.9) * At the base of the Weeping Wall, this is the obvious crack in a flare immediately to the left. It has the added benefit of being one of the only climbs in the shade through mid-morning. **Pro:** to 2 inches. **FA:** Bob Lindgren, Ed Evans, and Dick DeRusha, August 1970.

3. Blade Runner (5.12a) ** Tricky to lead, but great fun to toprope. After the first few moves of *Warm Up,* reach right and lieback the steep arête past three bolts to a 3-bolt anchor (50 feet). **Pro:** to 2 inches. **FA:** (TR) Bob Gaines, September 1986. **First Lead:** Steve Sutton and Clark Jacobs, December 1991.

Buttress of Cracks—Upper Right Side

Paisano Pinnacle

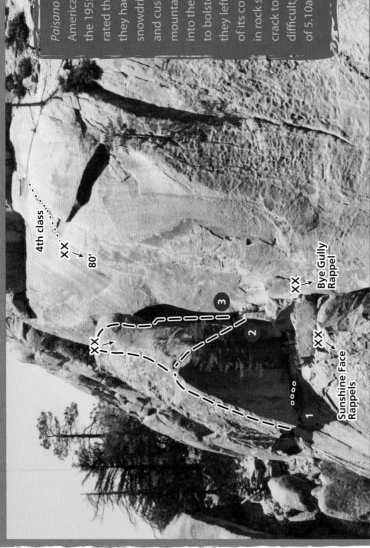

Paisano Jam Crack may be America's first 5.10. However, the 1955 first ascent party rated the climb 5.8, although they had distinct advantages: a snowdrift to shorten the route and cushion their falls; lug-soled mountain boots, which fit well into the crack; and a jug of wine to bolster their courage, which they left on the summit devoid of its contents. Sober climbers in rock shoes have found the crack to be considerably more difficult, thus the current rating of 5.10a.

4th class

XX ← 80'

3

2

1

XX

Bye Gully Rappel

XX

Sunshine Face Rappels

Paisano Pinnacle

13.

Paisano Pinnacle

Paisano Pinnacle is an amazing 50-foot-high block perched on Paisano Ledge atop the Sunshine Face. Part of its base juts out over the Sunshine Face, forming a roof. The *Paisano Overhang* climbs the crack that splits this roof. This same crack cleaves the entire pinnacle, and the *Paisano Jam Crack* route climbs the crack on the opposite side of the block. The easiest approach is up *Bye Gully,* or up any of the Sunshine Face routes that end at Paisano Ledge. It can also be accessed from the top of the cliff, by a short downclimb (exposed 4th class) down a smooth slab that slants down to rappel bolts directly above the pinnacle. This rappel (80 feet) ends on Paisano Ledge.

Descent: There is a bolted rappel anchor on top of Paisano Pinnacle (80 feet). From the extreme right end of Paisano Ledge, you can rappel from bolts down the *Bye Gully* (165 feet, or 100 feet plus 4th-class downclimbing) to the notch behind the Buttress of Cracks. From here it's a 3rd-class scramble down to the base of the Weeping Wall.

1. Paisano Overhang (5.12c) ***
Although John Long has dismissed it

as "an insignificant boulder problem," it is significant in that it was one of the first routes in America to receive the 5.12 grade, and since then it has repelled more than a few attempts. Jam the horizontal 4- to 5-inch roof crack overhanging the Sunshine Face. Once you turn the lip, the climbing eases considerably. **Pro:** to 5 inches, including several 4 to 5 inches; a #2 Big Bro is recommended after turning the lip. **FA:** (5.7, A3) Pat Callis and Charlie Raymond, January 1968. **FFA:** John Long, 1973.

2. Paisano Jam Crack (5.10a) * Jam the 4-inch-wide crack on the inside face of the block. **Pro:** to 4 inches. **FA:** Mark Powell, Don Wilson, and Frank Hoover, February 1955.

3. Wise Guys (5.12b) ** A unique climb that requires a full-body stem to reach holds on the inside face of the pinnacle. Stem the wide chimney behind the pinnacle. Once established on the face, move left around the overhanging arête (5.12-), then up a very delicate (5.12-) face. 5 bolts to a 2-bolt belay/rappel anchor (80 feet). **FA:** Bob Gaines, Kelly Vaught, and Frank Bentwood, August 1999.

The Weeping Wall

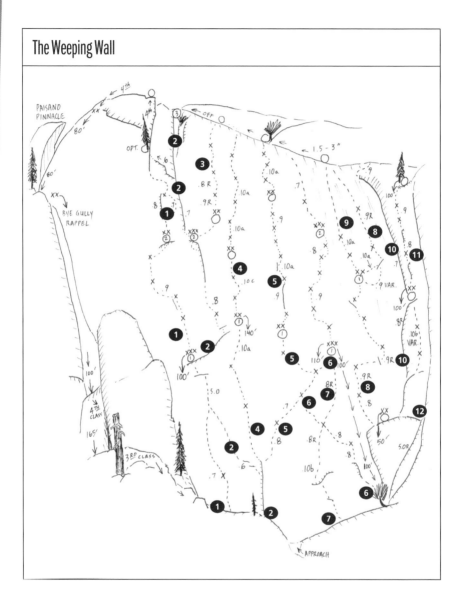

14

The Weeping Wall

The 300-foot-high Weeping Wall offers an assortment of the best moderate multi-pitch slab routes in Idyllwild, ranging in difficulty from 5.8 to 5.10. They are almost entirely bolt protected, and careful routefinding is required since the slab is riddled with bolts on closely spaced routes. Most of the belays have tiny stances or are hanging, with bomber 2- or 3-bolt anchors. The Weeping Wall faces southeast and is in the sun until late afternoon. In the summer months it goes into the shade about 3 p.m.

Approach: Where the trail up to Suicide Rock first gains sight of the rock, you'll come to a fork in the trail. Take the right fork, which winds uphill about 200 feet to the base of the Weeping Wall. The deep chimney on the left side of the face is the *Bye Gully* route (5.5), which is used to approach Paisano Ledge and is also the lower part of the standard descent route for the Weeping Wall.

Descent: *Bye Gully* **Rappel:** From the top of the Weeping Wall, walk left to where you can see the summit of Paisano Pinnacle, then head down a smooth slab (4th class) to reach a bolted rappel anchor. Rappel 80 feet to Paisano Ledge. At the far right-hand corner of the ledge (toward the Weeping Wall) is another bolt anchor. Rappel 165 feet (or 100 feet plus some 4th-class downclimbing) to reach ledges, then downclimb (3rd class) to the base of the Weeping Wall.

North Side Trail: To avoid any rappelling or downclimbing, walk up and right on slabs for about 300 feet until you reach a hiking trail (the Deer Springs Trail). Head right on the trail until past the North Face of the rock, where the cliffs of Suicide Rock end. Cut right off the hiking trail and down a steep slope, then head right around to the base of the North Face.

1. Clam Chowder (5.9 R) ** **Pitch 1:** Begin about 20 feet left of *Surprise*, then climb straight up the low-angle slab past a bolt to a nice belay stance with three bolts (100 feet). **Pitch 2:** Wind up and left, then back right, past four bolts to another bolt anchor. **Pitch 3:** Climb past two bolts (moving right toward the arête), then head left to a crack with a pine tree. Follow the crack to the top. **FA:** Jay Smith, Bruce Foster, Jim Wood, and Clark Jacobs, May 1973.

2. Surprise (5.8 R) ** The first climb done at Suicide Rock and a classic introduction to Suicide Rock face climbing. Start just left of the center of the slab. **Pitch 1:** Lieback a slippery right-facing corner (1.5-inch CD) for about 20 feet, then move up and left on friction (5.6) to easier (5.0) but run-out climbing up to the 3-bolt belay stance shared with *Clam Chowder*. **Pitch 2:** Traverse up and right on a ramp, then move up past a bolt (5.8) to a right-facing corner (0.5- to 1-inch pro), then left on the face up to a belay stance at three bolts. **Pitch 3:**

Step left and climb a flared crack that turns into a chimney. Be careful not to knock off loose rocks from the top. **Pro:** medium nuts, CDs from 0.4 to 2.5 inches. **FA:** Pat Callis and Larry Reynolds, April 1966.

3. Surprise Direct (5.9 R) ** Pretty bold for 1966! On the end of the second pitch of *Surprise,* clip the anchor for pro, then climb up and right to a higher bolt anchor and belay. **Pitch 3:** Climb a sustained slab past three bolts (5.9 R) up to the top (gear anchor). **Pro:** to 2.5 inches. **FA:** Pat Callis and Mike Dent, August 1966.

The Weeping Wall

4. Duck Soup (5.10c PG/R) ** **Pitch 1:** From the initial corner of *Surprise,* climb directly up the face past two widely spaced bolts (5.10a) to a bolt anchor (140 feet). **Pitch 2:** (5.10c) A short pitch past two bolts leads up a faint, orange water streak to another bolt anchor. **Pitch 3:** (5.10a) Climb past five bolts up to the top (gear anchor). **Pro:** a few CDs from 0.4 to 2.5 inches. **FA:** Marty Woerner, 1971.

5. Revelation (5.10a) ** **Pitch 1:** Start on *Surprise.* At the top of the right-facing corner, head up and right (5.8) to a bolt, then go up and right and clip the third and fourth bolt of *Serpentine*'s first pitch, then head up and left past one more bolt up to a bolted anchor (35 meters, 115 feet). **Pitch 2:** Up a little seam/corner, then sustained edging past six bolts up to another bolt anchor (5.10a). **Pitch 3:** Climb past three bolts up to the top. Belay at a tree. **Pro:** to 2 inches. **FA:** Ivan Couch and Mike Dent, August 1970.

6. Serpentine (5.9) *** Relatively well protected compared to its neighbors, this popular route meanders up one of the slickest slabs at Suicide Rock. Start from an oak tree up and right on a ramp from the center of the wall. **Pitch 1:** (5.8) Climb a short right-facing flake (medium nut) up to a bolt. The steeper left-facing corner just to the right of the flake is off-route (5.10-!). Traverse diagonally up and left past the second bolt. At the third bolt head up and right, past one more bolt up to a bolt anchor (105 feet!). **Pitch 2:** (5.9) Snake up the slab past six bolts to another bolt anchor. **Pitch 3:** (5.7) Continue up the slab past one more bolt to the top. Belay from a tree. **Pro:** a medium nut for the start. **FA:** Pat Callis and Lee Harrell, 1967.

7. Dire Straits (5.10b R/X) * Stay cool on the daring runouts, otherwise you'll find yourself in dire straits indeed. Begin between *Revelation* and *Serpentine* and climb over a small overlap (small pro here) past the second bolt on *Serpentine,* then directly up to the *Serpentine* belay. **FA:** Bob Gaines, July 1987.

8. Ten Karat Gold (5.10a R) *** The route originally sported gold-painted bolt hangers. This is the classic of the wall and not to be missed if you're a slab enthusiast. The rock quality is excellent. **Pitch 1:** From the oak tree near the right side of the face, climb the groove/flake that diagonals up and right (5.0 R), then move left to a ledge with a bolt anchor. **Pitch 2:** Head up past two bolts (5.9 R to the second bolt) and make a long traverse straight right (5.9 R) to the third bolt, then move up past two more bolts to a bolt anchor. **Pitch 3:** This is the infamous "window pane pitch." Traverse straight right (5.10a) or down and right (5.9), then up to the first bolt. It's nearly 40 feet up to the second bolt (5.9 R), then it's a stroll to the top (gear anchor). **Pro:** 1.5- to 3-inch CDs for the top anchor. **FA:** John Long, Richard Harrison, and Rick Accomazzo, June 1973.

9. White Line Fever (5.10a) ** This better-protected finish to *Ten Karat Gold* climbs straight up from the belay past two bolts to the top (gear anchor). **Pro:** 1.5 to 3 inches. **FA:** Clark Jacobs and Jack Roberts, 1982.

10. Sampson (5.9 R) * This route climbs the long left-facing dihedral

The Weeping Wall—Right Side

Godzilla Face

5.8 var.

Goliath 5.7

11

10

12

X·X

10

8

X X

12

that marks the right boundary of the Weeping Wall slab. **Pitch 1:** From the oak tree near the right side of the face, climb the groove/flake that diagonals up and right (5.0 R), then move left to a ledge with a bolt anchor. **Pitch 2:** Lieback a thin flake with sparse pro (5.8 R) to a 2-bolt belay at a small ledge. **Pitch 3:** Climb up the dihedral; where the corner arches left, make a crux (5.9) mantle to exit. **Pro:** thin to 2.5 inches. **FA:** Pat Callis and Lee Harrell, August 1967.

11. Bathsheba (5.9) * Begin from the bolt anchor on pitch 2 of *Sampson.* Climb directly up the arête past three bolts up to a belay at a tree. You can descend in three 100-foot rappels. **Pro:** to 1.5 inches. **FA:** Bob Gaines and Matt Bebe, June 2001.

12. David (5.7 R) * This route ultimately follows the spectacular arête bordering the right side of the Weeping Wall, with great views overlooking the Weeping Wall. Fantastic rock quality on the upper arête, but beware that this route has some largely unprotected climbing in the 5.6 to 5.7 range. Begin from the oak tree at the base of *Serpentine.* (See Rebolting Face topo, page 190.) **Pitch 1:** Climb an unprotected groove/

flake that diagonals up and right (5.0 R) to a ledge, then climb directly up the corner (5.5 R) or up and left then back right on easier ledges to a good stance at a small ledge. **Pitch 2:** Up a flake (5.7) just above the belay to the base of a huge chimney (*Goliath,* 5.7) where you can place a good piece of pro (2-inch CD) that still provides rather inadequate protection for the intimidating and improbable traverse right (5.7 R) across the overhanging right wall of the dihedral. Follow the crack (awkward 5.7), or step right and climb the wonderfully sculptured face of the arête just to the right (5.6 R), traversing over to and placing gear in the crack at several junctures. There is a belay stance at a tiny ledge near the end of the crack (0.4 to 2.5 inches). **Pitch 3:** Climb an easy flake up and right to a 2-bolt anchor (the top anchor of *Rebolting Development).* Pitches 2 and 3 can be easily combined with a 60-meter rope, but you won't be able to see your second on the traverse. **Descent:** Rappel from here (three 100-foot rappels), or continue to the top (4th class) and descend via the North Side Trail. **Pro:** to 3 inches (mainly 0.4 to 2.5 inches). **FA:** Charlie Raymond and Pat Callis, June 1966.

Rebolting Face

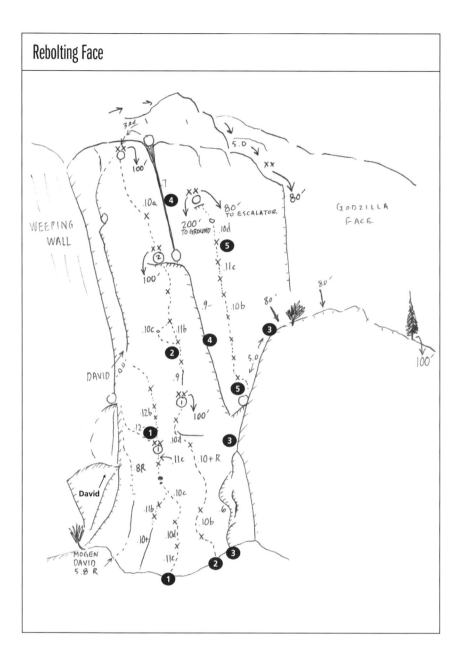

15.

Rebolting Face

Immediately to the right of the Weeping Wall is a massive, smooth, high-angle slab. Included here are routes up the main slab and routes just to the right (*Delila* and *Season's End*).

Just to the right of the main slab, a pair of rounded lieback flakes marks the start of *The Escalator,* which is used to approach *Delila, Season's End,* the Godzilla Face, and Sunkist Slab.

Rappel Descents: Established rappel descent routes are detailed in the individual route descriptions. From the top of the Rebolting Face, you can rappel *Rebolting Development* in three 100-foot rappels, all from bolt anchors.

1. Playing in the Freeway (5.12a/b) ** Extreme edging and smearing up an improbable face. **Pitch 1:** (5.11c) Tough moves right off the deck get you to the first bolt, then delicate and runout slab climbing goes past a second bolt, heading up and left to pockets (scary 5.10c) where a final bolt protects thin (5.11c) moves up to the anchor. **Pitch 2:** (5.12a/b) The original finish traversed straight left from the anchor (5.12-) to join *David.* A direct finish called *Reckless Driving* (5.12b) was added later, straight up a very thin face past four bolts, then moving left to join *David.* The *Diamond Lane Variation* begins just left

Rebolting Face

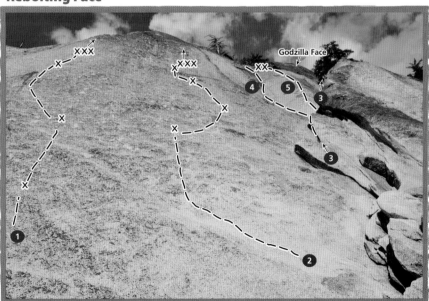

Rebolting Face Overview

of the regular start and climbs a thin crack to face climbing past two bolts (5.11b), joining *Playing in the Freeway* for its final bolt on pitch 1. **Pro:** to 3 inches for *David* finish. **FA, *Playing in the Freeway* and *Reckless Driving:*** Troy Mayr and Charles Cole, 1987. **FA, *Diamond Lane Variation:*** Dave Tucker, Mike Paul, and Paul Wilson, August 1987.

2. Rebolting Development (5.11b R) *** This face testpiece from the 1970s climbs the impressively blank high-angle slab located to the right of the Weeping Wall. It's entirely bolt protected, but it's no sport climb! **Pitch 1:** Start near the right side of the face. Smear past two bolts (5.10b), then make a long runout (5.10+ R) to reach the sanctuary of the third bolt. Traverse left and up to solution pockets (5.10d) and a fourth bolt that protects easier climbing up to a 3-bolt anchor. **Pitch 2:** Climb 5.9 moves up a little groove to a bolt, then go straight up to a second bolt that protects scary and thin moves (5.11b PG) up to a third bolt. It's possible to avoid the scary crux by traversing left at the second bolt to a knob tie-off, then moving back right (5.10c) to clip the third bolt. Easier climbing leads past a fourth bolt to a 3-bolt anchor at a small ledge. **Pitch 3:** Much easier (5.10a) friction and edging past one bolt leads to easier slab climbing up to another 3-bolt anchor. **Descent:** You can rap the route with three 100-foot rappels. **FA:** D. Wert, Mike Kaeser, and Greg Bender, October 1971.

3. The Escalator (5.6) This route is used as an approach and descent route to get to *Season's End* and the Godzilla Face. Follow a pair of rounded lieback flakes (5.6) for the first 25 feet, then climb up and right in a chute/chimney (5.0) that ends at ledges beneath the Godzilla Face. Often downclimbed to descend. **FA:** Unknown.

4. Delila (5.9-) * Climb the initial section of *The Escalator* and belay at the base of the obvious, huge right-facing dihedral. **Pitch 1:** (5.9-) Lieback the sustained, slippery right-facing open book up to a belay ledge. **Pitch 2:** (5.7) Climb a chimney to the top. **Descent:** From the top you can descend (exposed 3rd class) to the bolted rappel anchor at the top of *Rebolting Development* and descend in three 100-foot rappels. **Pro:** to 4 inches, including several 2.5 to 4 inches. **FA:** Pat Callis, Charlie Raymond, and Trish Raymond, January 1968.

5. Season's End (5.11c) ** A wonderful pitch of sustained slab climbing. Begin a short distance up *The Escalator* gully, just right of a huge right-facing dihedral (*Delila*). Climb past five widely spaced bolts on positive edges (5.10b), then crimp past three more closely spaced bolts on thin edges (5.11c), ending at a 2-bolt belay/rappel anchor. Some pro is useful before reaching the first bolt. **Descent:** Rappel 80 feet to the top of *The Escalator* and downclimb *The Escalator* (5.6), or rappel with two ropes (200 feet) to the ground. **Pro:** 0.5 to 2.5 inches. **FA:** Tobin Sorenson and Mike Graham (to the fifth bolt, then traversed left), early 1970s. **FA complete route:** Eric Erickson, 1978.

16

The Shadow Face

The Shadow Face is located about 50 feet right of *The Escalator*. From the Weeping Wall, head up and right for about 200 feet along the climber's trail, which leads directly to the base of the climb.

1. The Shadow (5.8 R) * A classic lieback. The flake has a positive, sharp edge for liebacking most of the way, until the crux, where the flake becomes rounded, necessitating a face move to the right. Up the positive but runout final section to a ledge, then head right on a ramp/flake to a belay/rappel pine tree (100 feet). **Pro:** thin to medium nuts, CDs from 0.3 to 3 inches. **FA:** Charlie Raymond, February 1968.

2. Free Lance (5.10c) * Lieback up *The Shadow* for about 15 feet, then traverse right (5.7) to a bolt. Climb straight up the slab past three more bolts (5.10c) to the ramp/flake of *The Shadow* and go up and right to the belay/rappel pine tree (100 feet). At the third bolt you can go straight up (5.10a) or right then back left (5.9) to the last bolt that protects the crux. **Pro:** small to 2 inches. **FA:** John Long and Brian Pottorff, November 1971.

Godzilla Face

Godzilla Face

The Godzilla Face is an unusual formation consisting of a slab capped with two monolithic blocks that form overhanging lips. *Godzilla's Return* and *Motezuma's Revenge* involve a combination of slab climbing and committing mantle moves.

Approach: The approach is via *The Escalator* route.

Descent: Downclimb (easy 5th class) to a 2-bolt anchor located on the left side of the Godzilla Face, about level with the first belay on *Godzilla's Return*. An 80-foot rappel takes you to the base of the Godzilla Face. From here you can downclimb *The Escalator* or scramble (3rd class) down to the pine tree rappel anchor on top of *The Shadow* (100-foot rappel).

1. Godzilla's Return (5.10d R) ***
Pitch 1: (5.10d) Climb the slab past three bolts and belay on a ledge (gear anchor). **Pitch 2:** Press out the infamous "Toad's Lip" mantle, which is most easily accomplished to the left. At the first bolt, either climb straight up (5.10d R) to a second bolt that protects easier

(5.10a) climbing up to a ledge, or climb up and left then back right (5.9 R) to reach the second bolt. The *Arête Variation* (5.10b R) to the second pitch starts at the first bolt and climbs up and left, paralleling the arête on the left, past one bolt (5.10b R) up to the same belay spot. **Pitch 3:** (5.10b) Up the face of the upper block past two bolts to the top. **Pro:** to 3 inches. **FA:** John Long and Hooman Aprin, April 1972. **FA, Pitch 2 Arête Variation:** Dave Evans and Margy Floyd, July 1989.

2. Mecca Godzilla (5.11a, A1) **
The aid on this route has thwarted free climbing attempts by some strong teams over the years. Start near the center of the face. **Pitch 1:** Climb the slab past two bolts to an overhang, where one bolt is used for aid, to a two-bolt belay stance. **Pitch 2:** Climb a thin face (5.11a) past two bolts, move left to a right-facing corner, and then up to a nice belay ledge. **Pitch 3:** Climb the upper block past one bolt to the top. **Pro:** thin cams to 2 inches. **FA:** Scott Erler and Paul Wilson, 1988.

Godzilla Face—Right Side

3. Montezuma's Revenge (5.10b R) *** Another bold classic from the "Stonemaster" era, with the pro well beneath you when you make crux moves. Begin at the right margin of the Godzilla Face, at the upper right side of the lower slab. **Pitch 1:** Lieback into a left-facing corner that arches left. Undercling left until the flake ends, then step up over the flake (5.10b PG) and climb up to a little corner. Move up and right (5.8) on a knobby face to a belay ledge. **Pitch 2:** A bolt down low provides rather inadequate protection for a scary and tricky mantle (5.10a R) over the lip of the overhang, then traverse right to a bolt that protects easier but runout climbing to the top. **Pro:** to 3 inches. **FA:** Tobin Sorenson, Gib Lewis, and Jim Wilson, 1973.

4. Baby Cobra (5.11b) * Begin on the far right side of the face, at the upper right margin of the lower slab. Start just right of *Montezuma's Revenge* and stem a left-curving dihedral (5.11b) with two fixed pins, then up a slab past a bolt (5.10a) to the belay shared with *Montezuma's Revenge*. **Pro:** thin to 3 inches. **FA:** (5.10, A1) Alan Nelson and Karl Mueller, 1978. **FFA:** Darrell Hensel, Dave Evans, and Todd Gordon, July 1986.

5. Komodo Corner (5.7) * This route climbs cracks along the right side of the upper blocks. Although the pitches are short, the jamming is good, and it deserves more traffic than it has gotten over the years. **Pitch 1:** Jam a hand crack through a slight overhang. Belay at a ledge at the base of a dihedral. **Pitch 2:** Jam the widening hand crack in the corner to the top. **Pro:** to 3 inches, including extra 1.5 to 2.5 inches. **FA:** Clark Jacobs and Jeff Best, 1974.

18.

Sunkist Slab

This beautiful white slab is located just right of Godzilla Face, and is most easily approached from *The Escalator* or from the top of the rock. The climbing is characterized by runout slab climbing on small, water-polished holds.

Descent: Rappel from the 2-bolt anchor on top of *Burning Down the House* (100 feet), or scramble (4th class) down the left side back to the base of the slab. ***Caution:*** Beware—there is quite a bit of loose rock at the top of the slab.

1. Question of Balance (5.10c R) * Begin at the far left side of the slab and climb a thin crack (5.10a), then move diagonally up and right (5.10c R) to reach a bolt. From here, climb up easier flakes, then a runout 5.6 slab to the top. **Pro:** thin to 2.5 inches. **FA:** Tobin Sorenson and Bill Antel, July 1973.

2. Cheap Day Return (5.11b R) * This is the hairline crack in the center of the slab, beginning just left of *Burning Down the House.* Climb the face on small, polished holds, using the thin

crack for pro (micro-nuts), then merge into *Question of Balance* for its top section. **Pro:** very thin to 2.5 inches. **FA:** (TR) Kevin Powell. **First lead:** Dave Evans and John Frericks, August 1984.

3. Burning Down the House (5.12b R) ** Another Darrell Hensel slab testpiece on water-polished rock. Considered by Darrrell to be his "most serious lead" at the rock, which is saying a lot. Climb the center of the slab past three bolts up to a 2-bolt anchor (100 feet). The moves from the first bolt to well above the third bolt are sustained 5.11+ or 5.12-, then a long 5.10 runout to the top. **FA:** Darrell Hensel, October 1987.

4. Jigsaw (5.10a R) Begin at the right side of the face. Climb a left-facing dihedral on the left (5.6) or a finger crack on the right (5.7), then up a face move (5.8) to a ramp. Clip a bolt, then up runout face (5.10a R) to the top. **Pro:** to 2.5 inches. **FA:** Tobin Sorenson, Bill Antel, John Long, Rob Muir, Richard Harrison, and Bruce Foster, July 1973.

Climber on *Hair Lip* (5.10a)
PHOTO BOB GAINES

19.

Hair Lip Face

Located about 75 yards to the right of the Weeping Wall, this face hosts one of Suicide Rock's classic arête climbs, *Hair Lip* (5.10a PG), not to be missed if you're solid at the grade.

Descent: From the very top of the Hair Lip slab, downclimb (4th class) about 20 feet down and right to a 2-bolt rappel anchor. Rappel with two ropes (150 feet) to the ground, or with one rope make an 80-foot rappel to the 2-bolt anchor

on *Step Right Up,* then another rappel (80 feet) to the ground.

1. Hair Lip (5.10a PG) ** This memorable and exciting route climbs the prominent arête just left of a gaping, flared chimney (*Hot Buttered Rump,* 5.10a R). Begin about 20 feet left of the chimney. A face move gets you to a thin flake; lieback this for about 30 feet, then make an improbable face traverse up and right (5.9) to

Hair Lip Face

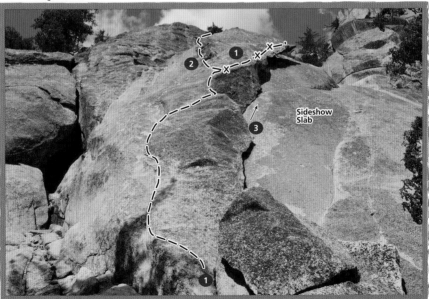

Hair Lip and Sideshow Slab Rappels

the arête and follow the lip of the exposed arête past three bolts to the top. The crux is above the third bolt, where a fall will send you over the lip of the arête. The top section involves a long runout, but the difficulty eases considerably. Belay at a pine tree. **Pro:** 0.4- to 1.75-inch CDs. **FA:** Ivan Couch and Larry Reynolds, October 1970.

2. Hair Face Variation (5.9) ** This excellent and less scary variation to *Hair Lip* moves left after the first bolt, face climbing (5.8) up to a juggy left-facing flake/corner that is followed until it ends. Move left, with a few face moves up to a thin crack, then follow an easy chute to the top. **Pro:** thin to 3 inches. **FA:** Unknown.

3. Hot Buttered Rump (5.10a PG) * This is the prominent flared chimney located on the left margin of the Sideshow Slab. *Hair Lip* forms the left edge of the chimney. It's a fun climb to toprope from the *Hair Lip* bolt anchor, but a bit of a horror show to lead due to a very loose flake wedged at the start of the chimney about 50 feet up, and somewhat dubious pro that must be placed awkwardly in the back of the flare. Begin by lieback-ing a right-facing corner (3- to 4-inch CDs) up to the chimney, which is most easily climbed by staying out in the wider section. **Pro:** thin to 4 inches. **FA:** Charlie Raymond and Lee Harrell, April 1968.

20.

Sideshow Slab

This mini version of the Weeping Wall is located just right of *Hot Buttered Rump,* about 100 yards right of the Weeping Wall. The climbs entail thin-hold slab and friction climbing on water-polished rock, which is sometimes wet early in the season.

Descent: From the top of the slab, make two 80-foot rappels (or one 150-foot rappel) from bolt anchors.

1. Step Right Up (5.10a) * Begin at the center of the slab and climb up easy

(5.0) ledges to a slab with four bolts (5.10a), moving right at the fourth bolt over to a 2-bolt belay/rappel anchor (80 feet). **FA:** Chris Miller, Pete Parades, and Cheryl Basye, July 1999.

2. Show Stopper (5.10a R) * Climb past the first two bolts of *Ours* (5.9 R), then move up and right and climb a smooth slab past six more bolts to a 2-bolt belay/rappel anchor. A less runout variation can be done starting up the left-facing corner crack on

Sideshow Slab

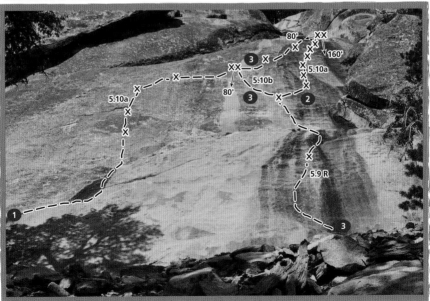

the right (5.7), then traversing to the second bolt on *Ours*. **Descent:** Make two 80-foot rappels or one long rappel (160 feet) to the ground. **FA:** Chris Miller, Pete Parades, and Cheryl Basye, July 1999.

3. Ours (5.10b R) * Begin at the right side of the slab and climb a slick, blackwater streak (5.9 R) up to a bolt. A 5.9 move above this leads to a ledge and a second bolt that protects the crux—thin-hold slab climbing up and left (5.10b) to a 2-bolt belay/rappel anchor. **Pitch 2:** (5.7 R) Up a slab past one bolt to a ramp with one bolt to a 2-bolt belay/rappel anchor. **Descent:** Make two 80-foot rappels or one long rappel (160 feet) to the ground. **FA:** Mike Graham, Steve West, and Alan Vick, October 1972.

Darrell Hensel leads *The Untickable* (5.12a)
PHOTO KEVIN POWELL

21

Eagle Pinnacle

This multifaceted formation is located to the right of and about 100 feet uphill from the base of Sideshow Slab. All the routes have rappel descents from bolts anchors. This area is in the sun until about 2:30 p.m. during summer, then is in the shade for the rest of the day.

1. Feeling Groovy (5.9) This is the obvious flared chimney just left of the *Untickable* that can be used as an approach pitch to set up a toprope. At the top of the chimney, move right on the ledge to a 2-bolt anchor (100 feet). **Pro:** thin to 3 inches **FA:** Bob and Yvonne Gaines, August 1987.

2. The Untickable (5.12a) ** Climb thin edges up the prominent buttress past six bolts, with the slightly runout crux above the fifth bolt, to a 2-bolt belay/rappel anchor (100 feet). **FA:** Darrell Hensel, July 1986.

3. Lichen Lovers (5.10a) * Start at the left side of the slab below *Razor's*

Eagle Pinnacle—Lower Left Side

Eagle Pinnacle—After the Gold Rush

Edge, and right of *Untickable.* Climb an easy corner up to a bolt, then move up and right to a mantle (5.10a). Cut back left then up edges and friction past two more bolts, with the crux (5.10a) at the very top. 3-bolt belay/rappel anchor (100 feet). **Pro:** three bolts, gear to 2 inches. **FA:** Dan and Debbie Haughelstine, August 1989.

4. After the Gold Rush (5.7) * Begin at the very base of the Eagle Pinnacle cliff, to the right of *Lichen Lovers.* Scramble up to a ledge at the base of a left-facing dihedral. Lieback the corner (5.6), then clip a bolt that protects a height-dependent move on slick rock over a bulge (5.7). Pad your way up a gold streak past two more bolts to a 2-bolt belay/rappel anchor (100 feet). **Pro:** to 2 inches. **FA:** Bob Gaines, Patty Kline, Kelly Vaught, and Frank Bentwood, June 2005.

Eagle Pinnacle—Lower Slab

5. Rhino Skin (5.10c) * Begin just left of *Finger Lickin' Good*. Fingery climbing on edges past two bolts (5.10b) leads to a short crack/corner, then friction past a third bolt (5.10c) up to a 2-bolt belay/rappel anchor (100 feet). Beware—the second bolt is a tough clip. **Pro:** to 2 inches. **FA:** Bob Gaines, Patty Kline, Kelly Vaught, and Frank Bentwood, June 2005.

6. Finger Lickin' Good (5.7) * A face move leads to a nice finger crack, ending at the communal 2-bolt anchor. **Pro:** to 2 inches. **FA:** Owen Gunther and Mark Minor, 1970.

7. Goblin (5.10a) * Start just right of *Finger Lickin' Good* with an unprotected face move (5.8) or up the easier crack farther right, to a friction slab with three bolts (5.10a). At the last bolt you can move left to the 2-bolt anchor (100 feet). **Pro:** to 2 inches. **FA:** Bob Gaines, Patty Kline, Kelly Vaught, and Frank Bentwood, June 2005.

EAGLE PINNACLE— UPPER SLAB

These routes are on a steeper slab, above *After the Gold Rush,* and are best approached by climbing *After the Gold Rush* or any of the lower slab routes, or by traversing left (5.4) from the far right side near the start of *Jizz* and *Spoodge.*

Descent: For *Kiss of the Spiderwoman, Razor's Edge,* and *Electric Razor* descend by rappelling from bolts 80 feet to the 2-bolt anchor at the top of *After the Gold Rush,* then rappel 100 feet to the ground. For *Schmooze, Jizz,* and *Spoodge* rappel 100 feet from bolts in an alcove.

8. Kiss of the Spider Woman (5.11b)
* From the bolt anchor on *After the*

Gold Rush, move left and stem the obtuse-angled corner past three bolts, then angle up and right to the 2-bolt belay/rappel anchor (80 feet). **Pro:** thin nuts, CDs to 2.5 inches. **FA:** (TR) Dave Evans and Jim Ivanko, October 1983. First Lead: Bob Gaines, August 1987.

9. Razor's Edge (5.9 R/X) Included here for reference, I can't recommend this climb because of the massive, fragile flake that will come off one of these days, hopefully not when someone is pulling on it! Lieback the precarious, loose flake past two bolts, moving right to a left-slanting hand crack (5.9) that leads up to a ledge with a 2-bolt belay/rappel anchor (80 feet). **Pro:** two bolts, several 2.5- to

Eagle Pinnacle—Upper Slab

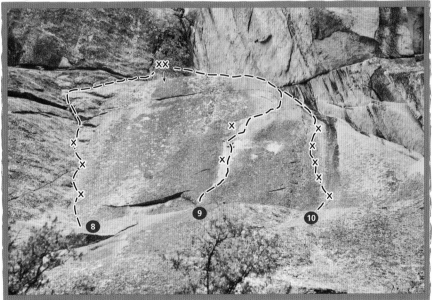

3-inch CDs. **FA:** Jim Wilson, Tobin Sorenson, and John Long, 1974.

10. Electric Razor (5.11a) * From the bolt anchor on *After the Gold Rush,* climb a sustained, thin face just right of *Razor's Edge* past five closely spaced bolts, then up the left-slanting crack to the 2-bolt belay/rappel anchor (80 feet). **Pro:** a few 2.5- to 3-inch CDs. **FA:** Scott and Robin Erler and Paul Morrel, August 1991.

11. Schmooze (5.12b) * This is a short, bouldery climb with challenging stemming located to the right of Eagle Pinnacle's upper slab and just left of the prow of *Spoodge.* Climb the slightly overhanging dihedral past two bolts and two fixed pins, then

up easily to an alcove with a shared 2-bolt belay/rappel anchor (100 feet). **Pro:** thin to 2.5 inches. **FA:** Bill Leventhal and Bob Gaines, July 1989.

12. Spoodge (5.10d PG) * Climb the tricky thin crack/groove up the prow of the buttress past a bolt and fixed pin, then up easily to the shared 2-bolt belay/rappel anchor in the alcove (100 feet). **Pro:** thin. **FA:** Eric Erickson and John Long, 1978.

13. Jizz (5.10c) * This is a short face climb on the right side of the buttress, to the right of *Spoodge.* Climb a tricky face past three bolts, then zoom up to the alcove with the shared 2-bolt belay/rappel anchor (100 feet). **FA:** Dave Evans and Todd Battey, 1989.

Eagle Pinnacle—Right Side

22

Northeast Buttress

The sheer cliffs of the Northeast Buttress possess some of the very best crack climbs on Suicide Rock, and probably the most famous one: *Flower of High Rank* (5.9), not to be missed if you're climbing at the 5.9 grade.

Approach: The Northeast Buttress is located about 200 yards right of the Weeping Wall. Follow the climber's trail at the base of the cliff past Eagle Pinnacle, where the trail climbs uphill a short distance to the base of the highest section of the Northeast Buttress, directly below *Flower of High Rank,* easily identified as the thin crack on a steep wall with a pine tree growing out of it about 100 feet up. To get to *Johnny Quest, Flakes of Wrath,* and *Rock Hudson,* traverse left on 3rd-class ledges about 100 feet to the base of these routes. The North Face is the massive, 200-foot-high slab with numerous exfoliating flakes to the right of the Northeast Buttress.

Descent: For routes that top out, walk right across exfoliation slabs to where the cliffs end, then follow a rough trail (the North Side Trail) down the slope that curves back around to the base.

Tony Sartin on the *Flower of High Rank* (5.9) PHOTO GREG EPPERSON

Northeast Buttress and North Face Overview

1. Johnny Quest (5.10b) ** This route can be easily identified by its classic finger crack that splits the upper half of the pitch like a surgeon's incision. Although the crux is short, this is one of the best 5.10 finger cracks at Suicide. Climb (5.2) up a gully on the left, then traverse right to a ledge with an oak and pine tree. A direct start can also be done up a 5.8 crack from the lower right to reach this ledge. Lieback and stem a short but very steep dihedral to the finger crack, then to a ledge with a 2-bolt belay/rappel anchor on top (100-foot rappel). **Pro:** thin to 2 inches. **FA:** Craig Fry and Spencer Lennard, 1979.

2. Flakes of Wrath (5.11a) ** This is another one of the great Suicide

Rock cracks. Start a short distance down and right from *Johnny Quest*. A powerful lieback up a dihedral with a thin crack (5.11a) leads to a flake that curves left. Climb up to the ledge with a 2-bolt belay/rappel anchor shared with *Johnny Quest* (100 feet). **Pro:** to 4 inches. **FA:** John Bachar, Gib Lewis, Jim Wilson, John Long, Eric Erickson, and Tobin Sorenson, 1978.

3. Flake Out (5.7) **Pitch 1:** Begin at the base of *Flower of High Rank* and traverse left on easy flakes to a series of short, vertical corners, and finally a strenuous squeeze chimney (5.7). Belay at a ledge with a bolt anchor shared with *Johnny Quest*. **Pitch 2:** (5.6) Traverse left and climb a long, low-angle, right-facing dihedral to

Northeast Buttress—Left Side

the top. **Pro:** to 4 inches, including two 4-inch CDs. **FA:** Pat Callis, Charlie Raymond, and Trish Raymond, September 1967.

4. Spooky Spike (5.9) * **Pitch 1:** From the base of *Flower of High Rank,* traverse left on easy flakes, then climb past the first short vertical corner on *Flake Out* and belay. **Pitch 2:** Lieback a tricky thin crack in a right-facing dihedral (5.9, micro-nuts), then follow cracks leading up and left, taking care not to dislodge the infamous "spooky spike." **Pro:** very thin nuts to 2.5-inch CDs. **FA:** Charlie Raymond, Bill Burke, and Trish Raymond, December 1968.

5. Etude (5.11a) *** Elegant is a good word to describe the climbing on the crux—more delicate than powerful. **Pitch 1:** Begin just left of *Flower of High Rank* and climb slabby thin cracks on the left until it becomes feasible to traverse right over to two steeper cracks, then jam a finger crack up to a 2-bolt belay/rappel anchor at a stance (125-foot rappel). **Pitch 2:** Jam a steep finger crack (5.10b) to easier climbing up to the top. **FA:** (5.8, A2) Larry Reynolds and R. Wendell, September 1969. **FFA:** John Long, Rick Accomazzo, Richard Harrison, and Tobin Sorenson, 1974.

6. Flower of High Rank (5.9) *** Perhaps the best 5.9 crack climb on Suicide Rock, and certainly the most popular, this steep route climbs the thin crack that splits the right side of the Northeast Buttress and has a pine tree growing out of it about 100 feet up. Climb up a gully (5.2), then lieback the thin crack on the left wall and jam double cracks up to a tree (5.9). Above the tree (optional belay hanging below the tree or standing on the tree with gear above it), either jam straight up the crack in the corner (5.8) or move out right on an exposed, right-slanting hand crack that leads up to a small roof. Turn the roof by reaching left to a crack (5.9, take care not to get your rope stuck in the crack), then follow easier (5.7) climbing up cracks and flakes to the top (gear anchor, 1- to 2-inch CDs). Can be done in one long pitch (190 feet) with a 60-meter rope. **Pro:** many from 0.5 to 3 inches. **FA:** Rob Muir and Mike Graham, October 1972.

North Face Overview

23

North Face

The North Face of Suicide Rock is located at the extreme right end of the crag, where the cliff diminishes in size before ending a few hundred feet to the right. The routes generally follow exfoliating flakes and cracks, with some great slab pitches in between. The left side of the North Face is bordered by the steeper Northeast Buttress (with the *Flower of High Rank*).

Approach: From the Weeping Wall, walk right on the climber's trail that follows the very base of the cliff for about 250 yards.

Descent: From the top, walk right across exfoliation slabs to where the cliffs ends, then follow a rough trail down the slope that curves back around to the base.

1. Graham Crackers (5.6 PG) * Begin 30 feet right of the start of *Flower of High Rank*. **Pitch 1:** (5.5) Climb a corner with semi-loose flakes up to a nice belay ledge on the left with two bolts (110-foot rappel). **Pitch 2:** (5.6 PG) Move right and climb thin flakes to face climbing up to a corner. Climb

North Face—Left Side

the left side of a down-pointing block, then move right up a crack through the slight overhang and up a short slab to the top (gear anchor; 1.5- to 2-inch CDs useful). The first half of this pitch has poor protection (the flakes are loose), but the crux is well protected with solid rock. **Pro:** to 3 inches. **FA:** Don Lashier and Trish Raymond, April 1968.

2. The Guillotine (5.8 R) ** Start from a large pine tree (fir) with an oddly curved trunk, where two massive blades of granite rest ominously at the base of the cliff. **Pitch 1:** Lieback flakes to a point where the main flake widens into a chimney. A committing lieback ascends this flake (5.8 R; several disastrous leader falls have occurred from here) to where the chimney ends and protection again becomes available. Make a few tricky moves, lieback about 20 feet higher, then move left to a small ledge with a 2-bolt belay/rappel anchor (130 feet). The runout lieback can be avoided by squeezing inside the chimney for pro, but this is extremely awkward. **Pitch 2:** Up and right in a crack, then up a slab (5.6) to the top. **Pro:** to 3 inches. **FA:** Allen Steck and Chuck Wilts, October 1969.

3. Superfluous Bolt (5.10a) * Begin about 25 feet right of *The Guillotine.* **Pitch 1:** Climb up to an overlap, then move left over it to a bolt. Climb up and left (5.10a) to a thin crack on the left side of the small roof, then up and right to a shallow, low-angle, left-facing dihedral corner and a bolt. Continue up to a shallow, low-angle dihedral, past a bolt, and up to a belay about 50 feet higher in the corner. **Pitch 2:** Finish the corner, then up a slab to the top. **Pro:** to 2.5 inches. **FA:** Ivan Couch, Mike Cohen, and Mike Dent, early 1970.

4. Obscured by Clouds (5.10d PG/R) *** A fog rolled in the day of the first ascent. **Pitch 1:** Climb past an overlap (5.9) up to a second larger overlap. Most climbers go left and clip the bolt on *Superfluous Bolt,* but the first ascent team avoided the bolt, climbing straight up to the overlap. Load up the crack under the overhang with gear (thin nuts and CDs), then bust crux moves up onto the slab and up to a bolt (5.10d PG/R) where a fall will send you sliding back over the roof. Climb up (5.10c) to another bolt (the *Shine On* finish goes straight up from here), then go up and right (5.9) to a 2-bolt belay/ rappel anchor at a quartz dike (100 feet). **Pitch 2:** (5.10a). Climb unprotected face moves up to a small flake (thin pro here), then easier friction leads to the top. **Pro:** thin to 2.5 inches. **FA:** Mike Graham, Tobin Sorenson, and Gib Lewis, 1974.

5. Shine On (5.11d PG/R) *** From the last bolt on the first pitch of *Obscured by Clouds,* climb straight up

North Face

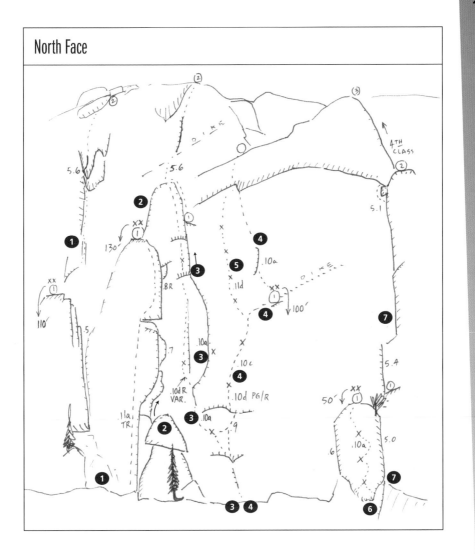

a smooth slab past four more bolts, with the crux getting to the second of these bolts. Cross over a roof at the top of the slab and belay a bit higher (gear anchor). This long pitch has seven bolts if you clip the bolt on *Superfluous Bolt,* and requires a 60-meter rope (200 feet)—a 70-meter rope is better. **Pro:** thin to 2.5 inches.

FA: Darrell Hensel, Mike Graham, and Ian Graham, September 2009.

6. Peer Pressure (5.10a) * A fun pitch of pure friction up the outer face of the slab just left of the start of *Tabby Treat.* 3 bolts to a 2-bolt belay/rappel anchor (50 feet). **FA:** Troy Mayr, Charles Cole, and Gib Lewis, 1987.

7. Tabby Treat (5.4) * This fun moderate route climbs corners on the right side of the North Face slab. **Pitch 1:** Climb the short right-facing corner (5.0) forming the right side of the *Peer Pressure* slab, past a stout bush, to a belay ledge up and a bit higher on the right (2-inch CDs). **Pitch 2:** Lieback a right-facing corner (5.4), then move right to a ledge (optional belay stance) to the main left-facing corner, which is followed to the top. Take care when passing a big loose chockstone near the finish. Belay at a ledge up and right (1.5- to 2-inch CDs). **Pitch 3:** (4th class) From here a low-angle slab leads to the top. **Pro:** to 3 inches. **FA:** Charlie and Trish Raymond, May 1968.

Darrel Hensel leads the first pitch of *Obscured by Clouds* (5.10d)
PHOTO KEVIN POWELL